# The Naval Academy—
# A Parent's Ponderings from
# Home Port

# The Naval Academy—
# A Parent's Ponderings from Home Port

## Untying the Bowline on I-Day

Steve Wade

Strategic Book Publishing and Rights Co.

Strategic Book Publishing & Rights Co., LLC
USA | Singapore
www.sbpra.net

For information about special discounts for bulk purchases, please contact Strategic Book Publishing and Rights Co. Special Sales, at bookorder@sbpra.net.

ISBN: 978-1-68235-620-3

# Contents

# LIFE ON THE YARD

# RAISING HEROES

## THE COVID CURSE

## ARMY-NAVY GAME

STEVE WADE

## A SERVICE SALUTE

# Dedication

To our USNA daughters, who were born sprinkled with sugar and spice and once donned buckles and bows. Though their hearts have yet to lose that which they were bequeathed at birth, their spirit is being honed as if by a warrior of the sea. They have taught my wife and me a few things along the way, included, but not limited to, character, integrity, and living life with a sense of purpose, and for that, we have become better people.

# INTRODUCTION

I recall the day our first daughter received her appointment to the United States Naval Academy. It was a day we had hoped and prayed for, and one our daughter had worked hard to realize. I was on the way home from work and received a call from my wife to share the good news. I was overcome with joy and I wept, hard. My eyes swollen with the sting of salty tears, I had to pull off the road to gather my faculties. My face had been declared a flood zone. I was grateful to be alone lest I embarrass myself. It was a feeling like none other. When our second daughter received her appointment, I was a bit more stoic. However, it is never easy to squelch the emotional tides which ebb and flow as we reflect on their journey along Stribling Walk.

There is one prevailing theme in this compilation of journal entries I hope will create a wake of introspection for anyone who has ever loved a midshipman or worn service dress blues on Worden Field. Our nation's finest young people, who have been invited to sit at the Naval Academy's grand table, are worthy. They possess the unique gifts needed to succeed there. When a cause needed a leader, they led it. When a game needed winning, they won it. When the school fund-raiser needed an extra push to reach their goal, they pushed it. And when their to-do list was simply impossible to complete, they completed it, on time.

The skills they bring with them, as wide as they are deep, will be opened wider and dredged deeper during their time under the watchful eye of Tecumseh. They amaze us all with their accomplishments, but never surprise us. These young people are our nation's future and for that, they deserve to be celebrated.

Induction Day will begin early and end late. As parents, the wheel of emotions will spin with no warning as to where it may stop. It is a day blended with joy, pride, elation, and a sense of achievement. At times, the wheel may stop along the avenue of dread, sadness, or a coming sense of loss. Untying the bowline and pushing our kids out to sea is never easy. When your plebe proclaims "I DO!" they belong to the Navy then. We relinquish the watch and commend our young prodigies to the caring hands of the Naval Academy. They will be fine and so will you. Just remember to bring lots of Kleenex and Shout Wipes. You will need the former and your plebe will need the latter.

Please know, as a parent, you are special too! You provided the ingredients to bake the magnificent cake you delivered on I-Day. Time is the currency your kids needed along the way. Without you, they would be bankrupt. Though those times you spent helping your high schooler work calculus equations proved scantly helpful, you did it because you knew they needed a cheerleader. Road trips with your kids to attend band camp, summer camp or sports camp were precious times spent together. You did it because you knew it was good and right. Hours of scouting trips, athletic tournaments, and recitals – you did it because you saw the value of the skills born from the effort.

Poking and prodding our children towards Annapolis is frowned upon, as it must be their decision to attend lest they be miserable living under the shadow of Mom and Dad. Though your job as a parent is never complete, the four years by the bay serve as a bookmark the Navy has carefully placed as a demarcation of where their watch begins and yours temporarily ends. You are encouraged to cheer, support, and pray for your kids. Though no one can care for your precocious ones like you, the USNA leadership and top brass do a really good job.

*Fair Winds and Following Seas*

# IF IT WERE EASY, EVERYONE WOULD WEAR WHITE WORKS

# It Takes a Different Kind of Kid

The navy blue, hard bound portfolio, when opened, presents a certificate that reads "The Superintendent of the United States Naval Academy takes great pleasure in recognizing with this Certificate of Accomplishment the selection of (insert name) for an Offer of Appointment to the United States Naval Academy with the class of (insert class)."

That is a big sentence full of opportunity and pride not easily swallowed in just one bite. For kids who have enjoyed this affirmation afforded by those words, which are strung together by threads of hard work and accomplishment, their buckets are brimming with promise to pursue their dream and a hope to fulfill it.

There is no guarantee, written or implied, that our precious dumplings will one day become Captain America. However, the genes you bequeathed, coupled with the Naval Academy's purposed plan to create commissioned officers who meet the pinnacle of moral, mental, and physical standards, are the ingredients needed to bake a superhero cake "imbued with the highest ideals of duty, honor, and loyalty."

CBS once said "It Takes a Different Kind of Kid." Truer words have rarely been spoken. Our children have made the decision to accept their appointment, knowing all the hard work, the risks, and the sacrifice. Doing hard things well is how they roll. They are signing up to lay down their lives to protect others they have never met, both foreign and domestic. When those massive bronze doors slammed shut, we knew Tecumseh now had the watch. Though the port from which they sailed will forever welcome them home, they have made a personal choice to moor their lives in Annapolis, four years by the bay, out from under the watchful eye of Mom and Dad. They belong to the Navy now. What once felt like ninety seconds to say goodbye on I-Day now seems like an eternity between visits. They are our heroes and ones we will forever cherish.

We have two USNA lovely ladies, one who threw her cover on high in 2019 and one who will in 2022. Both are our delight. We are blessed with their fervor, commitment, and will to serve. They are an inspiration to me and are becoming people I could never be. They are imperfect, have flaws, and sometimes get it wrong. Like others in the brigade, fleet, sky, and field, they are learning, as yours will, how to right the ship, steady the rudder, and set the sails, as the sailors and Marines they lead someday will depend on their knowledge, skill, and lessons learned while at the academy. We are blessed, as all us parents are, to have been invited to just sit along the roadside of USNA life and watch our kids endure the struggle that can come with N*ot College, participate in the joy of all its grandeur, and cheer loudly, without any shame, when they reap their enormous reward.

It really does take a different kind of kid...

# The I-Day Shake Down

Being bequeathed, and humbly accepting, the title of "Plebe-To-Be Parent" is not for the faint of heart. Wilting wallflowers need not apply. As our once-precocious tiny rock stars first climbed over the crib rail of life, most have earned a bushel full of success complete with trophies, medals, and have rarely met a letter south of an "A."

As doting moms and dads, we once hovered over our little dumplings as they belly crawled through the sandbox of childhood. We are the proud mamas and papas who cheered loudly, with our toes touching the sidelines, as we watched our budding athletes trip, stumble, and fall simply trying to understand which way to run. Dedicated to our parental craft, we insisted on standing ovations following their school concerts when unknown notes were played and tried not to giggle when singing in tune was not an option.

And we all knew that one *madre de familia* who managed the neighborhood carpool even a carrier Air Boss would envy. But, the best and bravest homework warriors amongst us pretended to know how to solve for "x," balance a chemical equation, or diagram a sentence as we knew special time together was the currency our children needed. Without our investment, they would become bankrupt.

Wait! What was that? It sounds as if the record needle, which has played such sweet music for oh so long, is losing its groove along the platinum record our gold star offspring have been spinning on their whole lives. For some of the incoming plebes, this will be the first time they have ever looked left or right and met someone just like themselves. The pond just became a lot bigger, and the fish, much smaller. Senior superlatives have faded into the yearbooks of the past. The silver horse they rode in on has been put out to greener pastures. But that is okay. Mom and Dad, your kids are in strong and trustworthy hands.

I-Day is a day like none other. You will swell with pride; they might shrink in fear. You will hyperventilate when you see your child with no hair, or much less of it. They will be anxious, desperately trying to do it all right, but cannot. Your eyes will scan the sea of white works, their eyes will be "in the boat." When they first emerge as bona fide plebes, they may look dizzy, scared, or just plain confused as to how they arrived there. They will most certainly be different than the young people you left only hours earlier at Alumni Hall.

But rest easy. Although the trials of I-Day are challenging for some, and just plain gut-wrenching for others, your kids are doing the right thing, on so many levels. They have been invited to the table from which only seven percent will dine. Anything worth doing is worth doing well. "Pressure with a purpose" is a theme, and it works.

So, before I put away this ball of yarn I am spinning, you need to know how awesome YOU are! Although you have a pretty special kid, that kid has pretty AMAZING parents. I know your little darlings are smart, attractive, and sporty, but you are the one who gave them the ingredients to bake the delectable cake now topped with an appointment to the United States Naval Academy. Well done!

Once they march through those enormous bronze doors of what will feel like their forever home of Bancroft Hall, it is time for you to pull the anchor and head back to your harbor of origin. Your child belongs to the Navy now. Try not to allow the salty swill, which will well up, to walk the plank until you are back in the privacy of your car. Unlike me, do not embarrass yourself while declaring your face a flood zone in public. My wife and I sobbed all the way to Richmond once we untied the bowline from our first plebe. After untying the line from our second, we were dried out by D.C. Truth be told, it was harder for us than for them.

Our oldest, class of '19 (now a LTJG), and our second born, class of '22, are still best mates. Following the I-Day "shake down," a hug and a little encouragement from big sis, who was a firstie detailer at the time, did the trick. Our youngest is a firstie now and thriving like a butterfly. Your baby will too.

# The Journey of a Thousand Miles Begins with a Single Step

⚓

It seems as if someone of great importance is soon to emerge from behind those massive and imposing bronze doors of Bancroft Hall which just slammed shut. Perhaps the pope, the president, or a foreign potentate is waiting to come forth. When taken at face value, any haphazard passerby would wonder why hundreds of people are standing on the steps, like paparazzi, wielding iPhones pointing towards the shuttered front door of this massive granite building. It seems a bit odd. Out of context, his imagination would be unbridled, his curiosities untamed, and his mind would spin with anticipation. Should he be privy to the moments he just missed, which preceded this otherwise benign place in time, he would understand the significance of not who may walk out but the significance of who just walked in.

As the sun set on that benchmark I-Day, our firstborn, the one who taught us how to be parents, marched over the threshold and through the wardrobe into a magical place affectionately known as "Mother B." As those monstrous doors slammed shut, with my gut wrenched, I leaned over and whispered to my wife, "We no longer have the watch. She belongs to the Navy now."

Since their own induction day, the class of 2021 has not yet stopped marching. Each inch they have trod across the Yard, for the duration of their USNA tenure, has spun a thread so strong, the fabric of their call to lead men and women into battle will forever remain unfettered. Though they may have entered this sacred place as Lucy did in C.S. Lewis' "The Lion, the Witch, and the Wardrobe," they will march together into Navy-Marine Corps Memorial Stadium as Aslan, one who is willing to sacrifice their life to save others while demonstrating their strength to face the White Witch and win.

The journey of a thousand miles begins with a single step. Four years prior, parents, friends, and loved ones were invited to sit along Tecumseh's sprawling court, under his watchful eye, as he surveyed his newest recruits take that first step down the long blue and gold line. A thousand miles does not seem quite long enough. From the first day they entered Alumni Hall, anxious but willing to accept the call, to today, dressed in their Navy and Marine Corps best, they have emerged as men and women of great substance, with a galvanized will to win. Most importantly, their willingness to lay down their lives for the greater good of all those they took an oath on I-Day to serve and protect has not wavered. They said "I DO!" when so many have asked, "Who will?"

Parents, today is your day too. Soak it in, bask in all its majesty, and know the steps you have walked alongside your soon-to-be-commissioned officer have left indelible footprints in their soul that will guide them in their time of plenty and in want.

Congratulations class of '21! You have earned it!

# Behind the Big Bronze Doors

One of the most iconic scenes of I-Day that shook us to the core was watching our child march through the monstrous bronze doors of Bancroft Hall as the sun set on that historic and milestone day. Their last step over the threshold of this marble and granite fortress, which has provided and is providing them safe harbor for their four years, is the last step we saw as our plebe embarked upon a journey that forever shaped their minds, hearts, and character and further reinforced their selfless spirit to serve. This is why moments like this exist. As parents, we so dearly wanted to capture that last step as our watch ended and theirs began. The doors slammed shut. Our children were in the Navy now.

For us, it was the most gut-wrenching event we had ever experienced, but one we will always want to remember. It was a day where we spun the wheel of emotions but had no control as to where it may stop. We needed two hearts to contain the pride and joy which accompanied the pomp and circumstance as Tecumseh oversaw his new recruits. Some plebes looked confused, seemed disoriented, and made me wonder if they had begun to doubt their decision to accept their appointment. I believe parents realize they are needed now more than ever before. Reassurance is the ingredient of the day; encouragement, the seasoning of the moment. We watched our support shore up our own plebe's ship which had begun to list.

The induction day experience for coming classes will look much different than those in our rearview mirrors. I am saddened this year that plebe-to-be parents will not have their guts wrenched during this season of COVID separation, nor their emotional wheel spun nor feel the reverberation of slamming doors. They will miss the confusion, disorientation, and the questions which will swirl about. But let not your hearts be troubled. Being a two-timing USNA parent, I can assure you, your child is in the right place. They are just as significant. Just as capable. And just as ready.

Ceremonies do not define them. Their invitation to the table is rare and one of high honor. They have earned the white works and Dixie cups they will don on day one. As hard as it may seem to pull anchor and set them adrift while waving farewell from Gate 8 or some airport terminal, know your overachieving offspring has what it takes to succeed at the Naval Academy. They are in the best of hands (although we feel there are no better hands than ours).

I would like to share one of my favorite quotes that laid still the churning tide in my heart and calmed the swells of uncertainty that sloshed in my gut on the eve of I-Day:

"If the highest aim of a captain were to preserve his ship, he would keep it in port forever." – Thomas Aquinas

Untying the bowline of the ship your plebe is about to board may seem like an act of valor, but letting the rope go is really more an act of courage, trust, and love. We knew our girls were ready, even though we were not.

I still well up a bit at that which we experienced. I have many fond memories of I-Day, but this one pricks my heart more than most. I guess it is because I knew the significance of that moment or, perhaps, I knew how significant these young men and women are who disappeared through the wardrobe of a higher calling to serve our great nation with distinction and honor. Newly minted plebe parents, while your kid will have their "eyes in the boat" this summer, their heart will never forget it is you that gave them the courage to raise their right hand and say "I DO!"

# Rearview Mirror

Sam Elliot once said, "There's a reason the rearview mirror is so small and the windshield so big. Where you're headed is much more important than what you've left behind." Anyone who has ever loved a midshipman or worn the blue and gold might disagree. The rearview mirror is where we reminisce and cherish the memories we have made, reflect on the honorable effort our kids have put forth, and remember their days of dedication which brought them to this place. Though smaller, it is no less important.

Though I was not present in Annapolis today for official plebe/parent business, I felt obliged to immerse myself in the wondrous happenings that surrounded the Yard this weekend. Our firstie, a first set detailer, and I attended PEP Friday morning. It was hot, humid, and, like osmosis, my body ached after watching Major Antonelli, with force and determination, push the plebes through exercise evolutions not fit for anyone over the age of nineteen. The bleachers were packed with parents watching with a sense of awe that their kids could move and bend like that, but mostly, their hearts overflowed with pride. Beads of perspiration and those of tears blended into one wet mess. Instead of PEP, I am now calling it "The Sweat Along the Severn."

Reunions tend to be sweet, full of fragrant aroma and coveted by those who have been separated for a protracted amount of time. As military parents, we are now majority shareholders in the business of reunions. Watching our sailors and Marines push back from the table of civilian life to live, not for themselves, but for those they serve, are now the stocks we trade. Few will be the hugs that have been so familiar. The kitchen table, where bread has been broken together so many years, now has an empty seat. Grocery lists are shorter, laundry baskets emptier, and the balance on your credit card is a fraction of what it once was. But in all this, time together becomes more precious, memories more dear, and hugs a lot tighter.

As I stood aside Friday, watching along Stribling Walk, the anticipation was palpable. Tecumseh proudly watched over his court where the class of 2025 said "I DO!" only six short weeks ago (though it feels like six months). Parents, family, and friends scanned the crowd, hoping to soon see their one, the one they have prayed would make it to this day. I saw moms tremble with expectation, dads, with reticent hearts, melt like butter, and grandparents wait patiently as they knew their hug was coming. Tears of joy were the guest of honor and pride for who stood in the white uniform before you was the best gift you could hope for. This moment will never be forgotten. Never will the feeling subside. And never will there be another like it. If you missed it, that is okay – there are more reunions to come.

I remember our last goodbyes with our two plebes years ago. I was able to hold it together until we closed the car doors; Mom was not. To watch our girls walk away following that last "I love you" was hard. The hugs seemed tighter, longer, and more purposed.

As we slowly crept away from Bancroft, and their image became smaller in our review mirror, we began to realize the significance of what just happened. Our babies were becoming exactly who they were designed to be without reservation or coercion. They are midshipmen of their own accord. They earned their seat at the table and we were simply invited to share in the grandeur of it all. Though overwhelming at times, our hearts were at peace. They were being left in good and capable hands. Midshipmen are our nation's finest. We now get to enjoy the dividends of the investment we made in our children. Bravo Zulu, parents!

Though the windshield the class of 2025 looks through now is huge, our rearview mirror will remain a precious reflection of those we left behind. No matter the time or place, our prayers will remain faithful, our love steadfast, and, like a loved one who paces the lighthouse catwalk, we will forever remain vigilant as we watch for their return.

# The Hyperbole of Parental Therapy

Naval Academy life can be drenched with stress, dredged with fear, and will cause separation anxiety not known to anyone who has not donned white works and a Dixie cup on a hot July afternoon. On the other hand, being a plebe parent may be worse.

My wife and I have been in therapy since our first I-Day to unravel the emotions which welled up from the moment we abandoned our child at Alumni Hall. Following our departure from Gate 8, with our '19er still learning to salute in the rearview mirror, we sobbed water balloon tears all the way to Richmond. After being forced to leave our second born behind hostile lines, we ran dry the salty river of sorrow by D.C. Our therapist said that was progress.

Our two USNA daughters, once frightened caterpillars who knew not which way to run, are now flourishing. They are not only the source of our joy but also the reason why neither of us have fingernails. One is now an ensign, while the other, a youngster. The Naval Academy has been an exceptional harbor of learning and leadership development. We still visit on occasion. Leaving is not as hard as it once was. We are now good by the time we pass Worden Field. Our therapist is pleased.

As USNA parents, we all have great stories to tell. Some make us smile while others make us relapse. I-Day is not for the faint of heart. Wilting wallflowers need not apply, unless you are us, who were given a wilting waiver. All that is behind us now. We have two more years ahead of the Naval Academy less the fear, stress, and separation anxiety. Never mind that last part. Our therapist says we still need work.

You have some pretty amazing kids. Let us covet their accomplishments. Shout their praises. Celebrate their commitment. Let us hoist up the class of 2020 and embrace the incoming class of 2024. The gift of parenting a midshipman is one worth stewarding well. Their anchor will be lifted one day and they will sail into the fleet and run into the field with the voice of their CO in one ear and the whisper of good parenting in the other. I want mine to be louder than theirs. Stress, fear, and anxiety need not apply for this mission.

# Superman's Phone Booth

The old saying "big things come in small packages" is an idiom that will be sewn upon every white work uniform on the Yard today. For the first time, since untying the knot from the safe harbor of home port, your big superhero will stand alone, privately, still in their small proverbial phone booth and dial the ten most treasured numbers they know at the moment.

This is their coveted opportunity to phone a friend and what a sweet privilege it is that you have been chosen, whoever YOU are, to bask in the presence of the one you love on the other end of the tin can. Just be sure to hit the little green button when the phone rings, not the red. A parent's anxiousness to hear their baby's voice can cause fingers to be a bit jumpy.

Being a parent who's received six of these calls, I can attest no two are alike, but the very first one revealed much more about myself than I was prepared for. Instead of listening, I asked too many questions. Instead of understanding, I strapped on my tool belt of clichés. Instead of absorbing and processing our plebe's emotions, I was too busy processing my own. I realized although our mission was to encourage, love, and reinforce the "why behind the what," I was so overwhelmed by it all I am sure our poor children were more worried about me than we could ever be about them. By the second call, they were fine, and so was I.

Our Navy girls now have a question and answer quota and I am okay with that.

Today is a special day – more special than most. Many of you have not been apart from your kids this long, thus grief has nested in your home. Plebe Summer is no day camp. Others believe separation is good and healthy and are thankful for the reprieve.

Today will reveal much: How your blessing, who was born to you all those years ago, has changed in a short fortnight. How they are transforming into the young man or woman you have hoped and prayed for (some more than others). Some are hurting. They are wounded. They are ready to ring the bell. The beach looks way better now than the shores of the Severn. Plebe Summer is hard. But it is worth the effort. It is worth walking over the finish line. Whether it be glorious or heart-wrenching, a moment in time does not define who they are. Although prodding our children to take the oath is frowned upon, prodding them to finish the race is encouraged. Swallowing that pill of discomfort and confusion can be painful, but the health and wellbeing it brings is just what the doctor ordered.

So, like diamonds and pearls have proven, big things certainly do come in small packages. Like Superman, that small phone booth your P2B precious gem walked into on I-Day will soon burst forth a bigger person, donning a large N* across their chest with an unfettered blue and gold cape boasting a big heart and an even bigger vision for service beyond self, to serve and protect those within our sovereign borders and beyond. Today is not just another phone call ... it is your superhero calling.

# Social Media: The Dopamine of USNA Parenting

As Facebook is the only social media habit I can manage at any one time, I tend to rely too heavily on Mark Zuckerberg to pacify my daily need for loves, likes, well wishes, and "atta'boys!" The daily dopamine game show of "What's on your mind?" is matched only by the goodness of the sweet tea cup sweating in my right hand. For most of us, our children are our most cherished "feel goods." Heaven forbid that piece of German chocolate cake you posted on Instagram last night garners more likes than the mug of your sweet baby who just won her first track meet. If so, you may need new friends.

My point? As a plebe-to-be parent, or one who is on their third exceptional child to wear white works and a funny cap, you have earned the gold star as the best parent ever to raise a son or daughter worthy of the "Facebook Post of the Month Club." I feel fairly certain I may have been unfriended a time or two over the years due to my less-than-humble ship's bow proclamations regarding the Naval Academy. My real friends just began commenting with an eye roll emoji and I was okay with that.

We have all been blessed to take a seat along the roadside of our kid's lives and just watch them harness life like only few can. There was a seven percent chance your offspring would be invited to the table of the United States Naval Academy. They overcame the odds because they set a goal to wear the blue and gold and were willing to do the work to don a Dixie cup cover on day one.

It is their journey now. We have raised them well. It is time to haul them to the Yard and let go of the rope. Some of us may feel as though it is a tug of war as we pull back on the braided twine which comprises all the goodness of our plebe-to-be hoping for one more hug, goodbye, or piece of parental advice. Our journey has ended in Annapolis – at least for now. We no longer have the watch. Our kid's eyes will soon be in the boat and on little else. "Pressure with a purpose" is the mantra that will rule the day. It is hard, but like our daughters have, your children have always chosen to do hard things, and do them well. That is why they will say "I DO!" and will so for the following nine years. It is a calling to a higher purpose and it is hard. It is just in their nature.

So, fire up Facebook and Instagram. Let the dopamine flow. You have earned it! Be a "top fan," "conversation starter," or the "visual storyteller" you have always wanted to be. However, if you begin seeing more eye roll emoji comments on your personal page, you may want to drop anchor and stay awhile with us friendlies. We love your children as we do our own. We are one big Navy family.

# Notes to the N*oteworthy

Putting pen to paper has become an archaic form of communication, and it is a crying shame. Much like the manual typewriter, ink designed to be laid down by hand seems to have reached its point of engineered obsolescence.

Fleeting are the days of beautiful cursive penmanship, when words once flowed across postcards and notepads with love, sweet as honey. Chicken scratch was discouraged, but acceptable. Merriam-Webster was a faithful spell checker and Wite-Out covered our grammatical sins.

I have noticed the ink pen aisle at our local Wal-Mart has shrunk a bit and stationery, like the morning newspapers which once donned our driveways, have become scarce.

Mailboxes have long forgotten the warm sentiments of handwritten letters and instead are now just depositories for cheap food coupons, unsolicited services and, Heaven forbid, a utility bill wiggles its way in there.

When our second USNA daughter, now a firstie, was muddling her way through Plebe Summer, although she has a precocious way about her, we knew written sweet nuthins of encouragement and unconditional support were necessary to prop up her listing ship when sinking seemed eminent (junk food care packages notwithstanding). Though we received three coveted letters from her, which are treasures still hidden away in our chest of drawers, I would like to think the bottled messages we dropped in the water washed up on her shoreline when she needed them most.

My papa pride says our party of pen and parchment pulled her through, but she would probably say it was the Cheez-Its and sour gummy worms we sent that did the trick.

I am thankful the Naval Academy believes in the value of handwritten notes and letters. It is an art form most of us have been the beneficiaries of but has since lost its place in our civil society. My hope is the exercise of letter writing will grab the fancy of our keyboard warriors who wear summer whites. One Forever stamp will make a forever impression.

As a kid from the time Garanimals were considered in vogue, I recall racing to the mailbox, which stood faithful through snow and rain, heat, and gloom of night, to retrieve whatever envelope had my name inscribed on it. I believe our college-aged kids still have the same craving to receive our written words when our voices are vacant. Of all we have to celebrate, our Annapolis dumplings by the Severn are ones which are certainly N*oteworthy.

Digital media is effective, efficient, and easy to access, but you cannot touch it, hear the crinkle of the paper, stick it on the fridge, nor can a text be stored in an old shoebox to be read years later. Time is of the essence, they say. "Don't blink," "time flies," and "before you know it" are all clichés which bear truth in the context of our fledgling officers. Our firstborn is now a LTJG. It was not that long ago the massive bronze doors of Bancroft Hall slammed behind as she marched in.

With all they are doing to prepare a life to be lived beyond themselves, place the needs of their own behind those of the sailors and Marines they will lead one day, and condition their hearts, minds, and bodies to fight the good fight to protect those who cannot protect themselves, the least I can do is dip my quill in the inkwell of encouragement and spread the following words on the stationery before me: "I am proud of who you have become and never forget, your Daddy is your biggest fan."

# Plebe-Parent Weekend: The Sweetest Reunion
## This Side of Heaven

Because my memory tends to slop around like an old wet mop inside a galvanized wash bucket, there are few things I can remember beyond yesterday's lunch. Sometimes this has rendered me paralyzed when called upon by my wife to bring forth important dates in our lives that not even the Dewey Decimal System could find. Only because of picture shakin' cameras and Super 8 film can anyone prove I was ever the mischievous child my mother said I was. Now, at 6'4" and tipping the scale just under the allowable weight limit of most commercial step ladders, the ballast in my mind equals that in my trunk. However, there is one memory which shook me to the core, and one I will never shake – Plebe-Parent Weekend.

There is simply no reunion on this side of heaven any sweeter, as if dipped in Godiva chocolate, than the moment your plebe, the child you birthed, reared, and set afloat along the Severn, appears from the sea of exuberant mayhem while wearing their new angelic summer white uniform. You may hyperventilate from excitement, but that is okay. It is expected. Fainting is not. Stoicism is in short supply on this day and big salty tears are encouraged to walk the plank of gratefulness as you behold who your son or daughter has become over the six weeks since you left them at Alumni Hall. The United States Naval Academy is presenting to you their newest and best for you to enjoy this weekend. It is as if your child has been born again.

But in all this, do not miss the moments. The moment when you embrace your child for the first time in six weeks. It will be a moment even a forgetful mind such as mine will never forget. Cherish the conversations. Take advantage of the tours. Relish in visiting Bancroft and going "on deck," a "top secret" place parents rarely see first-hand. Visit PEP at 0600 – you will be glad you did. Walk the Yard, engage together, and hug a lot. Buy gobs of NAVY spirit gear, feed your plebe well and often, and say goodnight only when you have to.

Take lots of photos. Like most of us, they will soon adorn your home, office, and social media. Also, take lots of time. Our youngest mid's "love language" is quality time. I believe your plebe might agree (at least this weekend) theirs is too. They need to know, no matter their circumstances, struggles, disappointments, desires, and successes, you have their six. There is no one who holds more dear the heart of your child than you. Certificates, medals, and trophies need not apply.

For those parents who cannot see their amazing kids this weekend, find comfort in knowing you have grown some of the finest young men and women this great country has to offer. Your children are among accomplished people who have their best interest at heart. We are one big Navy family. We take care of our own and we will take care of yours too.

Our second midshipman is a firstie now. I had to pry Mama Bear away from her sweet cub. Each of our two PPW reunions were a gift and ones we still display on our shelves and will always bear in our hearts. Bring boxes of Kleenex, Shout wipes, and lots of love, hugs, and kisses. You simply cannot over-deposit those.

26

Our family will be there this weekend too, but with our firstie to celebrate the retirement of her sponsor dad, a Navy Commander. I am sure we will reminisce a little about this day three years ago, when we too were spread out along Stribling Walk and Tecumseh Court searching across the sea of joy for one another. If I happen to stroll by, I will be the big guy holding the box of Kleenex under my arm trying not to hyperventilate while watching you all love on your kids.

# Summer Seminar: A USNA Vacation
## Along the Severn

My wife and I agreed upon leaving our girls in Annapolis for USNA Summer Seminar. "They'll either love it or they'll hate it." We were hoping for the former.

It was recommended to us our girls should apply for Summer Seminar if they had any questions about wearing the blue and gold one day, so they did. If I recall, they did so happily. We were told by little birdies who flit about the rumor mill that if candidates are extended an invitation to participate in Summer Seminar, it was basically an offer of appointment. As naïve as a left-handed smoke-shifting parent can be, I believed it! From that point forward, snipe hunting would have been more fruitful. I learned truth does not lie along the chatty sidelines of a high school soccer game, but more from the USNA mouths of those who make the rules. Though being accepted to attend Summer Seminar is not the golden ticket, it does play well with other accolades your superstars already bring to the admissions department round table discussion.

Of the ways to peer through the veil of America's most outstanding service academy, programs like Summer Seminar is one worth the application and effort to attend. It is a hard knock summer vacation but one which will shape your rising high school senior's position on hard work, perseverance, and determination. It is a fun week dripping with sweat, caked in mud and fear that coincides with living life outside their comfort zone. Perhaps it's not as relaxing as tanning by the pool, but tanning by the Severn includes a dash of boot camp blended with a whole bushel basket of fun. Three squares a day, a comfy rack, attractive USNA spirit gear, and creating new friends they may see again on I-Day are all good reasons to mark their calendars to gather on the Yard in June of each year. If navigating to higher education with a license to serve with a selfless heart, obtain a world class bachelor of science degree, and become one of our nation's newest superheroes, the Naval Academy is a wise first stop along the trail of becoming a bona fide leader.

The Yard can be intimidating at first blush, but its beauty softens the fear. The granite and limestone buildings can weigh heavy on an unsure heart, but the surety of their foundations props up the inner core of each person who visits and Tecumseh, who stands watch over his court, conveying a sense of strength as a warrior might once the battle is won. Why is this important? Because, like osmosis, when your kids step through the gates of the Naval Academy, they will see, feel, and know the almost two centuries of midshipmen who came before them, who charted a path towards service in the Navy and Marine Corps. It is a sense that will permeate their hearts and will lay pride on their shoulders. Like we thought about our girls, they will either love it or hate it. We decided either outcome would be acceptable.

So, if the Naval Academy seems like a good idea (and I can attest it is for the right candidates), Summer Seminar is a great place to start. Candidate Visitation Weekend (CVW) is also a viable option to step backstage to witness some of what it takes to produce such a performance. Best wishes and full steam ahead!

# LIFE ON THE YARD

# To Imbue

"Imbue" is not a word that typically flows from one's mind as they awaken from a night's slumber. However, as the first red cardinals began to share their morning gossip around the feeder, which I consider trespassing if before 0600, this word bubbled up without my permission to do so. It is a word that made my brain hurt at such an early hour which no pill or beverage could cure. It was as if a splinter had lodged into my cerebral cortex which I was now trying to pull free.

As I sat in my old and worn, but supple, leather chair that snaps and pops with the slightest movement, I begin to unravel this foreign word which I had never heard until our daughter first recited the Mission of the United States Naval Academy. It is the only word in the mission statement my simple mind could not process until I consulted Google for advice. I have since learned "imbue" is an "A-lister" kind of word.

To imbue something is to inspire or permeate with a feeling or quality. For someone who likes homemade biscuits like me, sausage gravy imbues my breakfast plate with creamy goodness. Well, sorta like that. In the case of our young, fledgling Navy and Marine Corps officers, the mission statement says it this way: "to imbue them with the highest ideals of duty, honor, and loyalty." Why not use simple words like "instill," "ingrain," or "infuse" for us more blue collar thinkers? Because the word "imbue" pushes the concepts of duty, honor, and loyalty to mine deeper into the core of who our mids are becoming. It is a dyeing of their spirit. They are being imbued to a selfless and sacrificial service which only they can now steward.

I found a photo of us attending a formal parade during our firstborn's plebe year. We were just so thankful she did not pass out, drop her bayonet, or march out of step. Mama was proud while I cried big salty tears. This was just a random shot in time, mostly because I was looking for our Waldo. I did not know ANY one mid in this photo, but I know EVERY mid in this photo. I may not know them by name, but I know what they stand for. Why? Because I have read their mission statement. "To develop midshipmen morally, mentally, and physically ... to imbue them with the highest ideals of duty, honor, and loyalty" matters to them. It will matter in the fleet and it will matter as they navigate the currents and tidal shifts of life after they serve. These words will be their compass through the shadows of trouble and guidance through stormy seas.

I covet their mission statement. I too want to be imbued with something as significant as duty, honor, and loyalty. Until then, I will be over here with my biscuits and gravy while admiring what the Naval Academy represents and just how blessed we all are to be a part of it.

# A USNA Kind of Day

The Naval Academy is just hard. It is hard to get in and it is hard to get out. I-Day is really hard. Plebe Summer is even harder. The Navy SEALs say "the only easy day was yesterday." Sounds rock hard. But midshipmen do hard things well. Their entire lives they have chosen not to approach life doing things the hard way, but instead, choosing to do the hard things in life, always with excellence. Though the preceding was jotted down in a previous journal entry, it bears repeating because truth is timeless.

Your precocious children have carried the torch, won the race, led the fight, bore the burden with strength, and have sought truth, honor, and integrity along the way. They have been a light on the hill when the darkness below seemed deep and unknown. They have a hunger to achieve, to motivate, and teach those who they lead. Each MIDN also has an appetite to learn, a coachable spirit, and is eager to glean knowledge from those who teach.

When rising to the occasion was needed, they did it. When losing was eminent, they won it. When classmates were in need of a leader, they led them. Midshipmen, though none are perfect, are the hope of our country's future. A student body "imbued with the highest ideals of duty, honor, and loyalty in order to graduate leaders" is the pudding of truth stirred into our superstars of today and America's superheroes of tomorrow as they prepare to fight in the field and fleet.

Living the big life on the Yard is not as glamorous as I once thought. Life there is not for the faint of heart. It is an early place, where birds that rise in flight as the sun peeks over the Severn are met by hundreds of kids, running, pushing, jumping, and rowing. Why? Because it is in the school's mission to develop midshipmen physically. It is also a late place where the midnight oil burns bright well after Colors settles over that hallowed ground.

Their days are long, time is short, and rarely are they idle. The to-do lists they manage are impossible to achieve in a single day, but they do. They have to, because tomorrow's tasks are just as important as today's. Learning is seen as an opportunity to do great things, meaningful things, things of significance. USNA is a place in time which proves timeless. The United States Naval Academy has provided a table of military honor and, with great consideration, has invited our nation's best to take a seat. It is a ship they will be taught to never give up and they will learn to damn the torpedoes.

I am a writer, not a fighter. I see words, dream up metaphors, and can spin threads until I am all tangled up. When I talk with our Navy children, whether in Bancroft or in the fleet, I hear their words, but I read their tea leaves. I also read their messages, but it is the lines in-between that interest me most. We like to keep the wire between the tin cans taut, but only as much as the Navy allows.

Below is my interpretation of a call we received during Plebe Summer a few years ago, but a call anyone could receive when our collective offspring are in uniform. Our USNA superstar was no longer the big fish, big dog, or Big Kahuna. She was less than. The least among these. The last one, and she was feeling it.

Her ship was listing and her sails had flopped. Things were hard, but she needed hardening. "Developing midshipmen morally, mentally, and physically" takes guts, courage, and virtue. I was reminded again, the Naval Academy is just hard. Here is what our plebe really wanted to say, if she could – you know, because I can read the tea leaves...

"Today was a fight. An offensive lineman kinda fight. A suplex, tap out and bloody MMA kinda fight. The kinda fight where high sticks are legal, knees and elbows are not fouls, and a hit by pitch is expected. At every turn, my day teetered on the precipice of the next disaster. The what ifs, why fors, and what coulds flooded my emotional carburetor. I'm exhausted. If I were a drinker, I'd need 'one bourbon, one scotch, and one beer.' But because I'm a fighter, I fought the good fight. I did not win every round. Those I did win were sprinkled with determination and grace. Those I did not were laced with lemons, but I found lessons. My muscles ache, my feet hurt, and my brain feels mushy. William Wallace would be proud. So would Jesus. My strength to push plows in hard clay came from Him. Otherwise, I would've lost this metaphorical battle crouched on the defensive line ... on the first snap."

Ours made it! And so will yours.

# Movement with a Purpose

Midshipmen do not fiddle-faddle, loaf, or lollygag. It is simply not in their DNA. "To solemnly swear to support and defend the Constitution of the United States against all enemies, foreign and domestic" requires a gut greater than one who just piddles about.

Not once have I visited the Yard and seen anyone in USNA issued threads of pride and freedom move without a purpose. To "imbue them with the highest ideals of duty, honor, and loyalty in order to provide graduates who are dedicated to a career of naval service" is the main ingredient found in the recipe of purpose.

After leaving behind our oldest daughter, now a LTJG, for a candidate visitation weekend, I remember thinking, "If we went to war, these are the kids I want to stand behind." More importantly, the shoulders of these USNA midshipmen are ones I so dearly wanted our daughter to stand on. The United States Naval Academy is for the selfless-minded with a warrior soul who believes life has purpose and has chosen USNA to help fulfill it.

# Small, But Not Insignificant

Most of us cannot begin to fathom how vast and deep the oceans are that envelop this mysterious planet upon which we live. Every molecular drop of saline-tainted water that fills the cracks and crevices along the shorelines of our nation, and of every other nation, both friend and foe, is sovereign in the eyes of those compatriots who can dip their toes in it.

I recall a photo, captured of our mid daughter in Memorial Hall inside Bancroft, which stirs in my heart a sense of smallness amongst the cavernous limestone, granite, and tile dormitory, but not one of insignificance. As she, and others like her, pull anchor and bear their headings across newly chartered seas which at times can seem more bipolar and less predictable, a sense of smallness can be a commodity not too hard to find. However, as vast and deep as the oceans are, so too is the community of men and women who, as one unified force for global good, are on watch for you and me.

My heart reminisces… Let me be the crevice into which the ocean fills so my soul will know not the emptiness of a life less lived. May a sense of smallness transform into a humble heart and the angry sea that swirls and swells find peace within my hands who sail it. Tame the currents, man the battle stations, steady the rudder – we have toes to protect and foes to put asunder.

# This Is No Costume

Though it is Halloween, the men and women who form on the field for game day do so not as characters in costume but real heroes in the uniform of the day.

There are no tricks under the watchful eye of John Paul Jones, Tecumseh, or Mother B. No shortcuts to be found, no handouts, free candy, nor participation trophies. Our Navy, nor Marine Corps, travel door-to-door requesting aid. They are there to offer it, to guard it, and to meet the needs of those who need it.

The backs of those in formation are donned with clothing worn by our nation's finest. These uniforms, as if the armor of God, are worn not out of reluctance to duty, but to honor their oath to uphold it. These mids want to serve; their hearts require it. Though their minds may question at times, their souls would be saddened if they could not.

So, applause all around as we cheer on our amazing children. Those Batman and Cinderella costumes they once wore on this haunted holiday so many years ago are now Summer Whites and Service Dress Blues. May their plastic pumpkins overflow with all that is good and right. Their service is a delight to watch, their sacrifice is unknown to most. They have earned their treats – porch peddling need not apply.

Happy Halloween, everyone!

# Girl Power

Once upon a time, girls had certain roles, roles different from boys. Roles with little danger. Pits of peril need not apply and forgone exploits which would never prove legendary. Though their spirit longed for adventure, their gender rendered them limited in their campaign to quarterback from the front. There were times when USNA commissioned females could not serve in the midst of war, or even take a quick joyride around the block aboard a naval battle-worthy ship. That which they studied and toiled over for their four years along the Severn did not pay the dividends congruent to their investment.

As Americans, we have so much to be thankful for, a bushel basket of which we owe to the men AND women who have toed the line in uniform. For those sporting two X chromosomes, I am especially grateful for the oars you have placed in the water as your extraordinary efforts have created a hydrodynamic lift for the ships you drive, jets you fly, land battles you fight, and all those under your command. The opportunities being afforded our daughters in today's theater should never be entitled, but earned. Deserved, not arbitrarily awarded. Being "imbued with the highest ideals of duty, honor, and loyalty" is not gender specific.

May the best man or woman win the billet, earn the pins, procure the patches, and climb the brass ladder as those above them reach back their hands to lift up those deserving to keep the watch when needed. Male or female, it makes no difference.

Both our girls held positions of leadership while at the Naval Academy alongside their male counterparts. They were not perfect, they failed at times, but served their little corner of the brigade well. I see our girls becoming someone I could never be. I will save the sap, but I am their biggest fan, not only because they belong to me, but because they have each carried a big sword on their hips, which I fear.

# The State of the Brigade is Strong

The Brigade of Midshipmen, whether they traverse the Yard, stroll through DTA, or march as one bonded entity not easily sunk, are a formidable passel of determination, grit, and service beyond self. They gleam like naval angels in their summer whites and ready themselves for the big gala when donning their dress blues which inspire confidence and leadership amongst those who sail in their wake. As CBS once endeared a nation to our children's endeavors, their statement, "it takes a different kind of kid," was a testimony of truth.

As a USNA parent, pride is never absent, awe abounds, and motivation to be our best selves flows from the Severn straight to our home port. Our closets are stuffed with spirit gear, cupboards listing with cups, tumblers purchased on a whim, and our vehicles papered in stickers, because the first two we stuck there did not serve as proper notice of our Naval Academy parental status. Wearing the blue and gold unapologetically is a privilege afforded to us by our children, and for that, I am grateful.

Our daughters, like their classmates, have dedicated themselves to something far greater than most who live outside the proverbial wire. They, and those of their ilk, said "YES!" when they were asked, "Are you sure?" Each appointment afforded is a challenge to grow, a decision to be better, and a commitment to serve and lead others on behalf of our great nation.

The Brigade of Midshipmen is a strand not easily broken. It has been said as those under your command grow, so grows your opportunity to serve those you lead. That is a slogan worthy of any conference room motivational poster. Our collective children share different leadership duties that transcend through those who bunk in Bancroft, but with one common purpose. Mids share a desire to steady the rudder in rough seas, sail their crew to safety when currents are strong, and correct course when storms ahead threaten their cause.

Like those they serve, who are also of like mind and mission focused, the state of the Brigade of Midshipmen is strong and a force to soon lead the fleet for global good.

# A Hall Fit For a King

⚓

Like most midshipmen, the ballast of their daily schedules, which can weigh heavy on any to-do list, requires a gaggle full of calories to keep their sails at full mast. Good food is essential for our overachievers. Their engines need fuel to navigate along the Severn and morale is known to be tied to tasty sustenance. At times, a quick snack is warranted as they briskly walk from post to post. Midshipmen rely on the Naval Academy to fill their bellies for success, and USNA does it well.

In most cases, restaurants do not mind accommodating large parties for a meal. However, some have their limit as to the walk-in business they will tolerate. In my experience, ten is typically the maximum before exasperation settles over the host and panic ensues while tables are pushed together and extra dinnerware is distributed like a blackjack dealer in Vegas. But, unlike dinner reservations for a family of four, USNA brings the whole battle group to the table simultaneously, most days topping out at 4,400 strong – per meal. Although I am no mathematician, my culinary calculations reveal a number north of 13,000 plates are being laid down every day and the mission is accomplished with military precision.

Christening King Hall in honor of Fleet Admiral Ernest J. King, USNA class of 1901, is quite fitting given his storied

Naval service and hero status as a flag officer and once Chief of Naval Operations. It is comforting to know our own midshipmen heroes sit under his legacy across almost 400 tables while they consume, on some days, 3,000 hamburgers or 2,500 pounds of chicken (roughly the weight of a Ford Fiesta). My mother would be so proud. If the sixth love language was feeding people, she would need two hearts to hold her joy should she be present to witness such a feast. However, washing approximately 40,000 pieces of silverware, dishes, and glassware following every meal should be left to the professionals lest a novice cleaning crew develop dishpan hands not even Playtex gloves could stave off.

I have been there. I have seen the controlled chaos that transpires as mids pour in, one by one, with full minds but empty stomachs. Meals are served family style within five minutes of taking their seats and many are walking out the door in less than thirty. There are nutritional goodies for every taste, diet, and caloric need. Some mids need far more calories than others which would cause a husky size guy like me to saunter about the dining hall asking my company mates "You gonna eat that?" In a typical day, the brigade consumes more than 1,000 gallons of milk, two tons of meat, a ton of green vegetables, two tons of potatoes, 1,200 loaves of bread, 700 pies, and (my favorite) 300 gallons of soft serve ice cream and fruit smoothies. Oh, my! As the sun sets and Colors echoes across the Yard, the kitchen staff is already planning for sunrise.

Because stories are often better told in person, be sure to ask your mid about peanut butter.

My gratitude for those who plan, prepare, and put forth quality food which sustains our children is immeasurable. Though it may not be like Mama's home cooking, it is good enough and served with determination and focus of purpose as the kitchen staff knows how important their mission is. Though our midshipmen are the heroes who receive accolades for their contributions, those who ensure our kids are fed are the unsung heroes who toil proudly behind the veil of wholesome greatness.

Three times every day, it is like manna from Heaven which falls for anyone willing to bend over and pick it up. King Hall is a blessing. It is a place I hope you can visit sometime, best if full of hungry hippos vying for that which gives them strength. My simple dinner prayer as a child was "God is good, God is great, thank you God for all that's on my plate." I would also like to add a BIG thank you to those who help make the savory ship sail and the mess hall sing with culinary joy.

This really is a hall fit for a king!

*King Hall food service statistic credits: Naval Academy Public Affairs Office (https://www.usna.edu/PAO/faq_pages/ KingHall.php)*

# Rough Weather Makes for Good
# Sailors and Marines

*A memorial to those midshipmen and USNA commissioned officers who now lay silent beneath the honor of their legacy.*

Like rough weather makes good timber*, rough seas make strong sailors and Marines.

In the wake of those midshipmen and USNA commissioned officers who have passed well before their time, I cannot help but remember the mainsails of our precious Naval Academy family and how they seemed to descend the mast of service much too soon.

As each Navy and Marine Corps officer does, our midshipmen begin and end their days with the proud and robust brass trumpet of Colors, an echo which reverberates promise throughout the Yard as the sun rises over the Severn to bid the night adieu and set again while tipping its hat to the waiting moon. Sadly, for a few of our precious children, their trumpet from which notes in honor of our woven tapestry of freedom flowed hours earlier tragically turn to the forlorn meter of Taps by day's end.

As their brothers and sisters do on that hot but honorable Induction Day, clad in their bleach white uniforms and Dixie cup covers, they pledge to uphold this oath in part: "I take this obligation freely, without any mental reservation or purpose of evasion; and that I will well and faithfully discharge the duties of the office on which I am about to enter. So help me God." And so they do, faithfully. With their selfless servant hearts packed deep in their core, they will be forever spun into the fabric of our Navy family, one that is not easily frayed.

As I have joined with our USNA family, hearts tattered, I cannot grab enough joy to soothe my soul when a piece of our grand puzzle is lost. We hurt. We grieve for the families of those who never reformed. Their navigational beacons have forever changed their course, not for the jetty of peril but the lighthouse of hope. We all have hope that good will come, somehow, from somewhere.

In the midst of adversity, as midshipmen faithfully do, the great young men and strong young women born of the brigade, both in the fleet and field, will rise to adhere to their oath, in part, to "support and defend the constitution of the United States against all enemies, foreign and domestic." And so they have, faithfully. Regardless of the circumstances, our lost will forever be on patrol. HOOYAH and OORAH!

As we endure the pokes, prods, and thorns of life, our hope is to gain wisdom, grow stronger, and love better. The Naval Academy is hard. The fleet, even harder. Wilting wallflowers need not apply. "Pressure with a purpose" is the motto of Plebe Summer. But goodness comes from rough and tumble, testing and stress, pushing and performing. Like the friction of a flowing river smooths the stones which nest beneath its surface, so too the storm that commands the swell to raise its shoulders and stirs its currents with its iron rod galvanizes our inner core.

The chaos strengthens our courage, hones our resolve, and smooths the rock of our souls. Although our beloved midshipmen have been relieved of their watch, their legacy of strength and honor will continue to nourish the seeds within us to grow strong and true.

I believe these words speak truth of our fallen and represent our midshipmen well...


Good timber does not grow with ease:
The stronger wind, the stronger trees;
The further sky, the greater length;
The more the storm, the more the strength.
By sun and cold, by rain and snow,
in trees and men good timber grows.
*"Good Timber" by Douglas Malloch*

*Opening quote: "Rough weather makes good timber" – Patsy Moore Ginns

# The Sunday Night Scaries

Perhaps our household constitution was a bit wilted, wrinkled, or wrapped too tight, but Sunday nights in our home have, for years, been haunted by the dread of its arch nemesis, Monday. The veil of uneasiness would typically drape our wonderful weekend memories around the dinner hour. It was a sight to behold, especially if an English paper was due the next morning. Woe be to those, such as Mama Bear, who dared spin the coming day with any attempt at positivity. Let the eye rolls and gnashing of teeth begin.

I will make this quick, as I know most of us have something more important to do than read a piece on how to avoid becoming a grumpapotamus.

Parents! Tomorrow is a huge day for our midshipmen: The first day of the academic year. For plebes, it is their first Naval Academy class ever. For firsties, their last first day of class. For some, somber. For others, pure joy. Tomorrow, the sail catches the wind, the rudder meets the tide, and the oil will begin to burn until midnight. Your kids, my firstie, are embarking on a world class education, one that only seven percent of those who apply are afforded. USNA is ranked, on average, in the top five schools our great nation offers to the best and brightest minds. Your child's name inscribed in gold lettering on the black bookbag they carry to class has been earned.

They will be challenged beyond their expectations, but not beyond their capabilities. There is simply not enough time in a day to achieve all they need to accomplish, but somehow, they will. They will be pushed, prodded, and their mind provoked to learn and retain more knowledge than they thought possible. But they must. This is N*OT COLLEGE; it is a sacred training ground to produce young adults of valor, moral strength, integrity, leadership, and sharp minds who can problem solve. These students are loyal to learning for the greater good of themselves and the nation they will serve and protect one day.

In light of the day that lies ahead, there may be some Sunday Night Scaries looming about Bancroft this evening. I am sure there is more than one mid ducking the drape of dread.

One of my favorite quotes from the movie "The Help," which we would recite to our girls, mostly as reassurance, was "You is kind, you is smart, you is important." I believe this is still true today. I wonder how many mids need to hear that, or something similar, to bring peace to their hearts and quiet their minds tonight? Perhaps just a whisper of a text will do.

Good luck and Godspeed to the brigade as they endeavor tomorrow to become the men and women they were destined to be.

# The Canvas

⚓

Someone once said, "Red sky at night, sailor's delight." Though I was never a sailor nor even a dock mate, I find great delight in the red sky moments of sunsets, as if I were a boatswain minding my vessel's bow while chasing the setting sun. If I were the captain of my own ship, long and grey, I would summon my soul's wit and heart's passion to a spot of inspiration each evening to advise my wandering canvas as to which strategic brushstroke to make or Naval story to paint.

Our USNA officers in training will one day be issued their own canvas to paint. Some days may resemble the smooth ways of Rembrandt, when tides are at ease. Others will be scattered under duress and living long days, reminiscent of Picasso's confusion, even on his best day. When seas become turbulent and sailors and Marines grow weary amidst the chaos of the fight or just the mundane days of service, our children will have learned to be the calm in the storm. Their training will guide their crew through not the bliss of the red sky at night, but the warning of a red sky morning.

Our Navy daughters are becoming courageous, warrior-minded officers I could never be. USNA is producing artists with the budding military talent to prod, teach, and mentor their squads, battalions, and maybe a whole fleet, in due time. They inspire those they lead as much as God's canvas, which spreads across the evening red sky, inspires me.

Because duty does not call me when the whistle blows, I can sit before the setting sun until it tips its hat to the rising moon. I will ponder and pontificate on the beauty which lies before me and think of all those deployed, those we know and those we do not, as they ride the bow of the ship they sail, fly through the heavens that spread wide and high, and those who reside in each camp protected by a wire that only the most courageous of us will cross. I pray that they too can see the setting sun as I do. Let their canvas always be a delight as they push back from their dock and head their compass into the night, which I cannot do.

I am grateful to all those willing to serve in my stead. I am grateful for your kids and mine who said "I DO!" when many others never did.

# Sweet and Salty

Being a dad of two XX chromosome midshipmen, one now a LTJG, I am no stranger to assertive young women. If you are a USNA parent in the 28th percentile, you too know what it is like to live with strong and determined female children.

We nicknamed our eldest "The Admiral," as she kept us square on what was, and was not, acceptable household behavior. Our second born, now a firstie, was deemed "Speaker of the House" long before she had aspirations of wearing the blue and gold. From the very beginning, my wife and I knew our jobs were in jeopardy, and we were expendable.

Our girls were a cup full of sugar and a whole lotta salt. They had the hearts of princesses with warrior spirits. We delighted in their successes and guided them through their failures. Wilting flowers they were not, but they bloomed wherever planted. I would guess all mid daughters are much the same. Each one I have met seem to be cut from the same courageous cloth and were hemmed in with a parent's wisdom and love.

There is a picture I have always been fond of in my shoebox of sentimentals. The scene depicts a little girl, maybe about five, pointing a stick, as if it were a sword, at one of her male counterparts on the playground with the quote "I'm not bossy! I have skills, leadership skills!! Understand?" I believe this moment captures the essence of all our Miss Navy and Marine officers to be. I tear up a bit whenever I see it as I remember the day in "T Court" when our firstie, at the time, held her own sword as a company commander. I knew, at that moment, she was made for this.

# Squared Away

As a USNA Dad times two, I can testify there have been few shades of grey bleeding through the walls of our home over the years. Black and white have ruled the color wheel of our lives. To toe the line is a lifestyle. To follow orders, a top requirement. Chits, liberty, and stripes are not granted without merit. They are earned. I know it seems a bit strict for civvy life, but our precocious military darlings have run a tight ship and accepted little less from their mother and me since they first donned their Dixie cups on I-Day. It was as if they had been anointed as Admiral Thing One and Two on that momentous day. We are thankful though. We are better parents now.

Uniforms are important. The Navy has high expectations for being squared away. Each mid has many to choose from. Like the Garanimals we once laid out for our children so many years ago, they always know which outfit to reach for on any given day. The Naval Academy can be quite fussy about being ship shape with mids strolling the Yard in clean attire – so much so that Shout Wipes and lint rollers are essential accessories every mid has tucked away for their summer whites or dress blues.

I recently dredged up some old photos of me in my fancy clothes on the Yard for a Sub Ball that made me chuckle. As mostly blue jeans, Carhartts, and boots litter my closet, sport coats, slacks, and tuxedoes are only unveiled from their mothball-stricken bags for special occasions. Buttons can be elusive for large fingers, such as mine, and near impossible to wrangle. My girls (one in a moment of displeasure, as we were late) watched as I struggled to affix one side of my coat to the other. I realize uniforms are not my thing. I managed well enough to pose for a picture, but was disappointed seeing that my sweet tea and gravy biscuit love affair had betrayed me and was causing my coat to buckle a bit. To each his own, I guess.

Having our youngster home during this COVID extended vacation has been a pleasure. However, I think she is missing lunch formation, parades, and wearing something other than pajamas to class. Well, that might be bending the truth just a little. However, I believe all our mids long for, on some level, the structure, competitiveness, camaraderie, and intellectual challenge the Naval Academy offers. N*OT COLLEGE is more than just a nickname. Quarantine can only last so long. If yours is like ours, she is adapting to a new normal, but she will be ready to slide back into the uniform of the day when the USNA ship sails once again and attack each day with vigor as only midshipmen know how to do. As empty nesters, we cherish having her home, but we are looking forward to eating Cheetos and ice cream on the couch again after she leaves.

# Signature Along the Severn

*"We are persons of integrity, we stand for that which is right..."*

As the tides churn and turbulent winds push against their hull with ill intent, it is only those Naval and Marine Corps officers imbued with the "highest ideals of duty, honor, and loyalty" who can raise their sails to harness that which means their vessel harm and garner good for those they lead.

Our 2/C daughter, who signed her two-for-seven today, delighted us with photos of this momentous event for us to treasure. It is without measure the joy we, as all USNA parents, feel upon receiving confirmation of such a milestone. It is a moment rivaled by little. Our children have accomplished that which we never doubted they would achieve. Now, we must find contentment in their decision. Although our minds may find favor with their future, our hearts desperately want to hold tight the chain that anchored them to our safe harbor for so many years. It is time they set course, point their bow, and sail to explore new seas and fight worthy battles.

"We are persons of integrity, we stand for that which is right..." is a profound collection of words inscribed on the scroll signed by those midshipmen ready to serve their country. Those words mean something. They matter. Those that sign this scroll have not done so of light heart but with deep conviction. They believe these words. These midshipmen embody the script they have committed to. These words mean doing hard things – things these future Navy and Marine Corps officers have chosen to do their whole lives. They have got this. They will soon have the watch, and we, as a nation, are safer for it.

# Dark Ages

Any midshipmen who lives in the 21412 ZIP code has served on the HOA board of "The Dark Ages." They have been members in good standing since their shoulder boards were void of stripes. They have been as faithful to their winter duty as the postal carrier who drops letters in our mail receptacles. "Neither rain, nor sleet, nor dark of night shall stay these couriers from the swift completion of their appointed rounds." In fairness to those who trod the hallow grounds of the Yard from January to the Ides of March as spring break commences, I would also ante up dense fog, low hanging clouds, biting cold, and sharp wind which blows mighty from the Severn as it cuts the Navy-issued fabric on their backs. "The Dark Ages" is not hyperbole – it is reality.

Though the lives of those who call the Naval Academy home abound, the showy tulips have laid bare, the oak trees have graciously shed their leaves, the birds who once sang with pride as if singing second are silent, and the sky shrouds those who walk below in a hue of gray. It is during these days when seeking shelter from the blah of life is necessary to feed a hibernating heart of a vibrant spring. Comfort food is more than just sustenance. Warm beverages are like a salve which melts their frozen limbs and a trusty treadmill is far better than a run along the sea wall. Unlike the sultry days of summer when a slow saunter along Stribling Walk is acceptable but sweaty, it is this time of year when a nip in the air requires a skip in the step to scurry to the next refuge from the cold. With that said, there is always that kid, perhaps yours, who wore shorts to school, regardless of the weather, and would never confess how uncomfortable they really were. Those are the ones who could not care less about the weather there. Bless their little hearts.

In my time visiting our mids, when the cold sank on my shoulders like an icy yoke, the wake of sweep boats, forced along the water with oars of strength, were absent. The sails of the Navy 44s are at ease as their days to tack and jibe have come to rest for a while. The only movement just beyond the seawall seems to be whitecaps which flash along the surface of the river. The Yard is still and quiet, but those who view life through an optimistic prism might say the Yard is at peace in a world which is anything but.

And then it snows! What once was a dim day flooded with gray becomes joy filled for our future Navy and Marine Corps leaders. Snowballs, snowmen, and snow angels, oh, my! As if Narnia had come to life on the Yard, the warriors who train there are like Aslan as they prepare to face our foes. As in the story, the White Witch never wins as long as our sons and daughters are on watch. The sacrifice they have pledged and their duty to protect those who cannot protect themselves lies just off their bow and over the hill. Their selfless acts of service are seen as the mids fan out through DTA where they lend their shovels and a helping hand to clear sidewalks, driveways, and porches for homeowners who adore those who wear the blue and gold.

So, as our children, who are born of amazing parents like you, prepare to BEAT ARMY and the exams that follow, though their eyes may be in the boat for the coming days, I wonder if their periscope is up searching the seas for the winter to come. My heart would say not, as being a fun-loving bunch, our mids are ready to tackle that which lies ahead and celebrate their spoils of the fall semester war. Our precocious dumplings are much more resilient than most and they understand the assignment they have been bequeathed. Come January, may they "DAMN THE TORPEDOES" and, no matter how blah life becomes, never, under any circumstance, should they forget "DON'T GIVE UP THE SHIP!" is not just a mantra. It is a lifestyle.

# Mid Handshake

Even after riding the coattails of our '19 and '22 around the Yard, like parental groupies, soaking in all that the Naval Academy has to offer those of us not in uniform, visiting this special place along the Severn has yet to become mundane, ordinary, or routine. It is simply an extraordinary place filled with extraordinary people.

It has been said we should choose our friends wisely as we are but a reflection of those who surround us. Those who graduate from this historic institution not only earn a bachelor's of science degree but also a Ph.D. in discernment. They have decided to choose the right venue and, after four years by the bay, they fully reflect the depth of that which George Bancroft dreamt of in 1845. He envisioned creating a legacy of an unparalleled education and a sense of unwavering naval leadership.

When visiting the Yard, after squeezing the blood from my mid's neck, there are two things I love to do. One is spend my right arm and left leg at the "Mid Store." The other? Just sit somewhere close to Tecumseh while we both observe his grand court. Sometimes, driving 300 miles north from my humble hometown to just talk with these kids makes me a better person. Wisdom is an attribute which grows stronger with time. After seven years propped up along Stribling Walk watching our girls grow there, I am much brighter than I once was. I have also proven I am much wiser too.

While indulging in the gift of parental oddity with the unbridled courage to stand under the watchful eye of Tecumseh and just say "hello" to any mid, usually plebes, who look as if they need one, I sometimes stumble upon a kid who I know, either a daughter's friend or one born to dear Navy parents we have met along our journeys to Annapolis. As I was recently scrolling through my phone's photos, I found one netted as a by-catch captured in a random photo which caught my attention. It depicted a firstie friend from our hometown approaching me as if he were on a covert operation, quiet and determined to catch my eye before I caught his. I was not expecting to make his acquaintance but glad he said "hello" as I was feeling like the new kid in the lunchroom.

The mid handshake is unlike most you will find outside the gates of this fortified naval base. It is sure, strong, and communicates a sense of security that can be trusted. While "eyes in the boat" means something to those who carry the burden of becoming officers of the high seas, mountains, and sky, "eyes on target" does as well, and I was his. With purpose and integrity, this young man initiated a greeting with me from my blind spot, but one I was thankful to soon see. He is planning to be a pilot and one who I am sure will always have his partner's six. In this self-serving world, this guy is proving himself to be selfless.

There is no awkward or limp fish who swim in the pool of proper manners at the Naval Academy. Both male and female are of equal effort when I extend my hand for our culture's customary greeting. It is a tradition even COVID cannot put asunder. There is respect, honor, and a sense of professionalism baked into each motion, a dying gesture which seems to be melting into fist and elbow bumps, especially among young people. I guess old fashioned letter writing has too, but the Academy is still working on that tradition.

I look forward to my next time on the Yard. A time when my mind's eye is fading and needs a little polishing. I am blessed, I suppose, to have an amazing family and loving friends who support and care for me. I am also thankful I have garnered enough wisdom to take advantage, when possible, to immerse myself amongst exceptional young people. I enjoy surrounding myself with those who have served and are serving with ribbons on their chests and gold on their covers. I do so with a humble understanding that I am not them, nor can I be, but that I can glean their greatness as inspiration to be my best self. Even if it is sometimes awkward wandering around, just Tecumseh and me.

# The Brigade's Missing Piece

As per our family's holiday protocol, our children choose a puzzle they would like to assemble while home on winter break. Over the years, as their shoe size grew, so did the number of pieces we found in each box. Somewhere between "Goodnight Moon" and when boys suddenly no longer had cooties, our girls would anchor their bow for hours and just float on the gentle tide of jigsaw bliss.

This Christmas, our battle plan remains unchanged. Our 2/C is home and already underway, loafing and piddling her way through a thousand pieces of broken art, soon to bring life to that which matches its creator's image. "DON'T GIVE UP THE SHIP!" and "DAMN THE TORPEDOES!" echoes in her mind each time she realizes her slice of puzzle sanity has run aground.

I cannot help but think our lives, like a large puzzle, are interwoven, dependent upon others, to complete an image carefully crafted by its creator. As if a shattered mirror can no longer bear the unfettered image of the soul who peers upon its pieces, so to the image of a puzzle makes little sense when precious pieces are removed from the box it once was a part of.

Whenever our Navy family is grieving upon losing a piece of the brigade puzzle due to an untimely passing of life, we diligently check the instructions for direction. There is not a quill, inkwell, nor a brilliant mind which can write the words to heal our hearts and mend our souls. The image on the puzzle box, as we knew only moments earlier, has suddenly changed. Seemingly, the final puzzle piece which breathes life into the artist's masterpiece has suddenly been removed. For me, as a parent, it is a piece I would search to rescue for the balance of my life, but I would know deep in my core it is a piece I would never find.

As the brigade reforms each semester and a piece is missing due to a loss of a midshipman, their image will not. Unlike a shattered mirror, our fallen's likeness will fully reflect their lives and the goodness it brought to the Yard. The example they modeled, which is in perfect step with the oath they took on I-Day, will forever encourage those who follow behind. Like the lead ship in any battle group, their heading is always true and rudder straight. Though our beloved mid's passing will be forever felt, I believe we will soon see the void which is left behind is less of a missing piece and more a piece left for others to borrow when they too seem to have lost a piece of their own.

We now have the watch. *Fair winds and following seas.*

# RAISING HEROES

# We Really Did Raise Our Heroes

As Mid parents, we have so much to be proud of. Our once little darlings who long ago dipped themselves, like strawberries, in the chocolate fountain of childhood are now a bit more aged and sophisticated, sorta like a beef tenderloin steak with celery root gratin, laced with goat cheese crumbles, shrouded in kale (but hold the kale, please and thank you).

It is well known the Naval Academy is brimming with shooting stars, rock stars, and superstars. I would like to share with you one such star who shall remain nameless because, based on the theme of this little thread, I believe doing so just seems like the right thing to do.

As a mid parent, I feel as if I am one big T-shirt that oozes the words "Some people never meet their hero. I raised mine." Kleenex please... the saline tears are beginning to rise from beneath my eyeballs.

I am all too eager to flaunt my offspring around town as if they were my prized lamb who just won the kindergarten overachiever award. I am a bragger, not a fighter. But my kid is not keen on kudos. There has to be at least one humble spirit who resides within the four walls of gloat nation.

As brevity is the soul of wit (neither of which I harbor), I will tread water as I arrive at my point. Being humble is as easy as playing football with a ten-pound watermelon slathered in bacon fat. We can see humbleness through the fog of self-centeredness lying just across the goal line, but getting there often means putting on our helmet of selflessness which often does not fit quite right so we leave it lying alone on the sideline.

My wife received a call today from her sister, who received a call from her civilian daughter, who received a call from a firstie friend, who found out from someone's XO, to inform us that one of our little dumplings, who once dreamed of becoming a nanny, was just named youngster of the 2019 fall semester! Wait! What? We thought to ourselves "Does the string attached to the tin can in Annapolis not have a direct connection to her parents in North Carolina?"

The more I chewed the cud of wonder as to how our inclusion in this wonderful cake batter of joy and surprise was overlooked, it became clearer. My being miffed began to meld into a new sense of pride. Not proud like a peacock. That is gaudy pride. But being proud of our mid for two very different but important reasons. I am sure it required a bushel full of hard work and a peck of gumption to achieve such an accolade. Who would not be proud of that? However, for me, us not knowing this wonderful news our midshipman had held close to her vest bloomed in me a greater sense of pride for what was not said than the actual accomplishment itself. A kind of humbleness not chiseled into my DNA.

I have learned a great lesson. People see when good comes to those they know and love. A wide net need not be cast to fish for compliments. As they say, "work hard in silence and let the success be the noise." I am grateful at my age that I can still learn from my children, even those who once wanted to be a nanny.

We truly did raise our hero.

# The Moment of Anticipation

There are few feelings which well up in a parent's heart that rival the anticipation of seeing our child's likeness as they promenade from behind the veil of airport security. We watch and wait, "welcome home" signs and flowers in hand. Onlookers must think we are rock star groupies. Well, in a sense, we sorta are. Mom's checking "Flight Aware" every minute on the minute. If you employ "Find My Friends" and "Life360" as if conducting kiddo search and rescue missions, watching your kids fly across the country is one more valuable tool needed in your covert operational arsenal.

There she is! My iPhone video speed seems too slow for a moment as if a dream is unfolding, but in reality, the time elapse seems to be moving too fast. Smiles, frozen in the moment, are the appetizers we share. As the main course of our sweet reunion, hugs and kisses, sprinkled with salty tears, heighten the flavor of our familiar fellowship. And for dessert? The simplicity of our mid's voice, which falls on a parent's loving ears, reminding us of by-gone days when conversations were not tethered by cables and phones. We could play their USNA stories, even of the most mundane things, on repeat in our minds and they would never grow stale.

Our '19, now a LTJG, and our '22 have upheld a Thanksgiving homecoming tradition in repose of the Severn. Sharp dressed, but no more ribbons and bows. She is squared away now, gold buttons and all. Oh, happy day! Like yours, I pray, she is home safe and at this moment still nestled in her bed, well past her normal muster time. It is a wonderful life.

Whether by air or asphalt vein, on the occasion when their shined oxfords cross the threshold of our home harbor, we celebrate their presence and rejoice in their company. Like nesting dolls, each visit reveals a new likeness, larger, wiser, and stronger than the last. We feed them well, love them well, and as we once did so many years ago, we watch as they nap on the couch. We pray for their future and immerse ourselves in the quiet moment with grateful hearts.

As firstie parents, our tenured hourglass is bottom heavy. Though the scales of time once tipped in our favor, the shopkeeper of swag is soon to call our Mid Store cards due. Because our fledgling Navy and Marine Corps officers are soon to enter the fleet and field, as our oldest sailor has, our annual lunch party reservation will be minus one. Though she will be missed, I am thankful for her service as well as her brothers and sisters who ready the fight in the theater on this Thanksgiving Day.

The moment of anticipation is one we covet, sometimes for months, perhaps someday, for a year or more. Our hearts flutter as we envision that first embrace. Our eyes twinkle as we reflect on days long in the rearview mirror when our homes were full of noise, our pantries stocked with snacks, all nighters seemed all too frequent, shoes of friends piled high by the front door, and games, recitals, and plays filled our social calendars all because our kids were worth our time and for that, their Naval Academy experience is the outpouring of our eighteen-year investment.

It is a beautiful thing you have done as USNA parents. The kids you have raised are exceptional, well rounded, committed to ideals larger than themselves, and are "imbued with duty, honor, and loyalty". Be proud! You have done good, Mom and Dad. Ever since that very first moment of anticipation upon introducing our newborn dumplings to our family and friends, we have much to be thankful for on this holiday of Thanksgiving.

# In the Shadow of the Anchor

Every evening, as I retire my tenure as CEO of another day, the lights in our home are relieved of their faithful duty, one by one. The moths, which enjoy basking in the light, and tiny insects that doddle about the window panes simply move on to their night time lair and wait for the coming day. Though our power meter spins like that of a hamster wheel, I believe a well-lit home conveys a gracious invitation to anyone who wishes to visit.

Our children, either by choice or by coercion, tend to live life in their parents' shadows. It is a safe place, of a familiar shape, provided for their protection. A place to find shelter from the day's trials and a pallet upon which to rest with an assurance they will sleep well through the night. Like butterflies from a cocoon, our little dumplings will one day emerge from beneath us, step timidly into the light, and wiggle their way to create a shadow of their own, one where they will invite those who need protecting a place to find refuge from the trials they face and a soft pallet upon which to sleep.

Last evening, as I was walking through my routine of laying low the lamps, chandeliers, and porch lights in our home before bed, with my wood floors moaning in protest as I trod over their bones, an image hung heavy on my eyes in a way I had not seen before. The anchor, which has been hung on our glass-adorned front door as if a medal on the chest of a naval war hero, has donned our porch portal for most of our two daughters' stay along the Severn. It has served our family well for seven years now. Though the anchor has been a nice nautical feature, jammed pack full of Navy spirit, it is the shadow through the glass that laid at my feet I noticed, unlike any other time, which raised the hairs on my neck and chilled my heart. The salty tears began to well up as I realized the anchor, which has stood watch all these years, is a beautiful representation of our midshipmen, and now, it is me who stands in their shadow.

The shadow of the shield they wield, which has been "imbued with the highest ideals of duty, honor, and loyalty," is one to cherish and worthy to stand under. Now, the Naval Academy is training midshipmen to be the safe shadow for those who need protecting, a place to hide when those they serve need a retreat from the day's toil, and will soon be the assurance for those who need a soft place to lay their heads when the wolf knocks at the door. Their familiar shape that will spread across the seven seas, the heavens, and the fruited plains will be guided by the oath they took which proclaims, in part, "I will support and defend the constitution of the United States against all enemies, foreign and domestic." That is a deep and wide shadow for our collective mids to cast, but it is a net they have been weaving together their entire lives. It is just who they are.

So, as this anchor continues to occupy its coveted spot and warmly welcomes those who care to cross our threshold, though the front is attractive and dressed in hues of white, it is the shadow it casts in the dark of night which reassures me that our kids, as well as yours, now have the watch.

# Is There Fear in the Unknown?

Some thoughts from when our now- LTJG was engaged in PROTRAMID following her youngster year...

Is there FEAR in the unknown? Perhaps. How about JOY? Less likely. Fear of that which could cause us harm can choke our capabilities and tether our talents. Like jumping from an airplane, public speaking, or trying to wrangle a gaggle of disobedient children after recess, the strength within us can be held hostage. What then could be said about finding joy in the unknown?

I am a dad of two little girls who once were just tall enough to reach my hand while learning to walk. I hold dear memories of a time when I was the puppeteer directing, ever so carefully, their next move. The strong one. Their hero. Larger than life. King Daddy-O! They were precious children who loved their dolls, story books, and bedtime tea parties. Our oldest was a "Little Miss Fancy Pants" who once insisted she wear a bathing suit, tutu, and rain boots to Wal-Mart. Her mother was okay with that, and so was I. Now, our young ladies have traded their Patsy Aiken dresses and patent leather Mary Janes for summer whites, dress blues, and patent leather oxfords.

As military parents, fear of the unknown, by most standards, would be expected. Top secret deployments, relentless training, sparse communication, unbridled duty to others, and sacrificing thyself are but a few. How can anyone find joy in the abyss of the unknown?

Our once pint-sized blossom, now just shy of six feet, spent last week underwater in a nuclear submarine, somewhere in the Pacific. The what ifs, what coulds, and why fors began to flow. We did not know, she could not tell. This week, Marine training, with real Marines, leather necks, devil dogs. Oorah!! Next week, who knows? Navy SEALs, the Blue Angels, or a secret invasion of a foreign country. But not likely.

Here is where the joy drowns out the fear. Fear is easy. It is normal. It is baked in. Under these circumstances, joy is not expected. It is a challenge, but it is there. We find joy in our daughters. We delight in their capabilities, character, and service to others. To me, they are the strong ones now, the ones who are larger than life, the ones who will one day reach out their hands to those they lead. My heroines! The unknown now represents excitement, adventure, growth, and opportunities afforded to only a few.

Sure, fear is swirled in there somewhere. It is the enemy's most popular weapon. The capstone of anticipatory anxiety. Worry and fear can overwhelm, but joy is full and complete. We find joy in our daughters by being of the same mind, having the same love, and being in full accord and of one heart with God who made them just how they are. A little sweet, a little salty, with a whole lotta fight.

# The Yard

I was recently on the Yard to hand over our 2/C to what would soon become a two-week time of solitude and reflection as she is preparing to join the second set Plebe Summer leadership team. For most of us, the responsibility of molding the new recruits sounds quite daunting and a task for those of great strength and character. Perhaps true, but mine carried a bucket full of angst through Gate 8, not for the mission that lie before her, but with the fear of having a Q-tip shoved up her nose to test her COVID-19 status. She was thankful the violation of her olfactory region only took ten seconds, although she said it felt like ten minutes. All the trauma in the drama soon melted away and she was ready to tackle the day.

After watching her pull anchor and shove-off for the next big adventure, I eased my pickup truck through the tree-lined streets of the Yard as covertly as a parent can while dripping in spirit gear with too many USNA stickers adorning my tailgate. The grounds were eerily still and quiet. While there, I couldn't help but reminisce of our days spent visiting our girls. It is a place where your heart will swell with pride as you consider your midshipman's achievements and that which now surrounds them. Their selfless sense of duty to country will mine the inner core of your parental soul. Although the immense blocks of granite, limestone, and brick form the veneer of this mighty fortress, it is the Brigade of Midshipmen who indwell the inner core of Bancroft Hall that form the foundation of leadership that will soon take command in the fleet and in the field. Being imbued with the "highest ideals of duty, honor, and loyalty" is not meant for wilting wall flowers.

Peering up Stribling Walk, ending with the two massive bronze doors that serve as the portal through which plebes begin their Naval Academy experience, made my heart stutter. All the feels of two I-Days rushed through my memory as if a tsunami had unexpectedly washed over me from behind. The emotional rainbow which once spanned from joy, pride, and admiration to anxiety and worry, sprinkled with a mild sense of loss as we watched our girls march away, hung again over Tecumseh Court. As salty tears began to well up, the only feeling that lingered in that moment was how grateful I was to have been given the opportunity to trod the same brick pavers over the years as so many young patriots have before me.

My hope would be all mid moms and dads can visit the Naval Academy at least once. But be forewarned, bring a big box to harbor all the memories you will make, a small one stuffed full of Kleenex, and your credit card for the Mid Store. You will be lucky to make it out less an arm and a leg.

Like Tecumseh, who stands proud as he watches over his court, the classes to come will one day stand watch over their own sailors and Marines. As I drove away, I was reminded there is something inherently different about this place. A place where great leaders are called, not prodded. They are developed, not entitled. Carry on, good and faithful servants. May your bow be strong and your rudder run true.

# Ponderings from Home Port

It does not take long, once our collective midshipmen cross the threshold of an otherwise "at ease" and clean home, to feel and smell their presence. Naval Academy kids are not shrinking violets. They naturally do things big, bold, and boisterous. Walls rattle, ceilings vibrate, and doors slam, seemingly for no reason. Pantries struggle to remain full, the fridge mostly sparse, and their stuff lies around as if it has no keel or compass. But, when that sea bag drops with such a thud, you know your precocious lamb is back in the loving port from which they once sailed.

I arose early from my slumber this morning. Our home is old so every step on the hardwood floor seems to awaken the squeaky bones of each memory we have made here. As my lovely wife and firstie lie sleeping, with only the light from my phone, I stumbled my way to the kitchen. I do not know why, but as I walked in and flipped on the light, I noticed our young Navy lady's house key resting on the rustic and well-loved red oak table where, as a family, we broke bread together for nearly nineteen years. My heart began to palpitate because her key reminded me of our sweet girl's forever connection to her true home port. My mind began to swirl as my thoughts spanned from Cheerios scattered on a high chair tray she could barely grasp to midnight high school English papers we thought she would never finish. Needless to say, a few salty tears walked the plank of memory lane. It is no wonder we never gave away that old faithful table. I guess to do so would have been like giving away a piece of our family's soul.

No matter our sailor's longitude, latitude, or which salt-stained sea she's floating on, or under, some day that house key will always allow her access to the home port from which she came. She is no longer ours alone. The Navy adopted her on Induction Day. However, we will take great comfort that this simple, seemingly mundane instrument of connection, when needed, will not only unlock the front door to the home that built her, but also to our hearts who once held her tight when sleep was not an option, nourished her hopes and dreams, and taught her how to be a lady first and a warrior second.

# It is Never Easy

⚓

And just like that, as if a contrail, which moves swiftly and with purpose across the bluebird sky, our mid pushed back her bow at early light and set sail back to Annapolis.

She is our second to don the blue and gold, but unlike the feeling one may have when waving away a friend, it is never easy to untie the knot you love from the bulkhead and toss it back towards the boat.

After four short but beautiful days with our little girl, who is now not so little, we find ourselves once again watching as she follows her bearing to pursue her dream of Naval service. From the dock on which we stand, watching, hoping, praying, as she sets her compass for things greater than she, we swell with pride as tears walk the salty plank and drip, ever so slowly, from our cheeks.

I guess these days are just practice for when the Navy or Marine Corps says it is time to go. We know not where, nor what time, or with whom, but we WILL know our midshipmen are ready to answer the call.

As I peer upon our daughter's neatly arranged bedroom, which has given our sweet girl refuge and rest for many years, I find peace in her capabilities and character to serve. It is mostly vacant now and we are okay with that, because we untied her knot from our safe harbor on I-Day several years ago and have, with as much courage as a parent can muster, tossed her rope back onto the boat.

*Fair Winds and Following Seas*

# Annapolis Angels

⚓

I once explained to a friend how midshipmen at the Naval Academy are paired with a sponsor family who voluntarily, without coercion or an hourly wage, pledge to make themselves available to meet any additional needs our mids may have while away at school. They provide a soft place to land after a tough week of "eyes in the boat" – a home cooked meal, free rides to and from, well, anywhere, and, without hesitation, these families share their lives as if they have adopted a new, homeless child. As with most USNA blessings which seem unexplainable to those souls not enshrined in the comings and goings of the blue and gold, I get the deer in the headlights look followed by "Well, isn't that nice."

As a seasoned mid parent, while I would like to brag, such as a proud peacock might, to my friends like a six-year-old who just won a game of Chutes and Ladders, I have long since lost the energy to try and explain what feels like rocket science to them. Anything beyond my name, rank, and serial number tends to get lost in the Morse code I seem to be speaking. It is hard enough climbing over the speed bump of why we would ever send our kids there in the first place. No, the Naval Academy is not a military boarding school for wayward high school teens.

The Kings have faithfully served as a sponsor family for both our daughters. This precious crew has been a well of peace at times for our weary mid parent hearts and a fountain of joy along their journey thus far. Commander King, their sponsor dad, is a Naval Academy alum and retired USNA aeronautical professor. His sweet wife, Sandra King, has been the best doting mom-away-from-mom our girls could ever have. Their three children have been like siblings.

So, what I am really saying is I am jealous. Jealous because I have not had the same opportunity to walk alongside these amazing shepherds of life as our children have. Raising my own blood is hard enough. Taking on another who's not of your ilk takes guts.

The Kings have been a huge blessing to our family and we are so thankful our precocious little dumplings, and others just like them, have such a glorious resource to help carry them through their four years in Annapolis. Sponsor families really do deserve their own national holiday. Thank you to all who have served in this selfless and loving role. I have spoken with so many sponsor parents, and they each say the blessings they receive far outweigh the sacrifice, which is really not a sacrifice at all.

# Waltzing with Raindrops

My wife and I are over the moon for our special Naval Academy ladies, as I know you are with yours. Though our children are different, we love them both just the same. One is disciplined, dedicated, and determined, while the other, like Ferdinand the Bull, is content simply smelling the flowers and following her soul wherever it may lead, but can be a tough and gentle leader too. They both wear their uniform well.

Whether it be by Old Navy or the U.S. Navy, it matters not to either as they know woven threads do not make the woman – their spirit does. They each have been known to waltz with raindrops that once formed puddles outside our home. We have watched them endure failure, embrace heartache, and learn from their mistakes. One has stirred my soul with discipline of purpose and the love she has for her friends and family. The other has inspired me with her courage, character, and determination to live her best life. Both are the delight of our hearts.

As USNA mid moms and dads, we all revel in our precocious offspring. We are a proud gaggle of parents who could stick gold stars all over our neatly clad children. Our officers-to-be deserve as many positive adjectives as a thesaurus could spit out. We embrace what we have made, because like any good chef would, we find joy in our carefully crafted culinary creation.

Our daughters are special young ladies and more alike than their actions may convey. Not like Dr. Jekyll and Mr. Hyde, but more like peanut butter and chocolate, which once paired together make for one pretty neat kid. Like your mid, they exhibit a plethora of transferable traits regarding the uniform of the day.

Although our collective mids are true to who they are, regardless of their orders, they are learning to navigate the tight rope of military life while harboring those attributes that netted their appointments. Either in their Navy whites or J. Crew civvies, your children, and ours, are blended with all the best ingredients to bake one big successful cake. Whether we know them to be a wandering Ferdinand, the caped crusader, or one who enjoys just waltzing with raindrops, they will always be our USNA heroes and we would not have it any other way.

# Thoughts from a Midshipman Dad

I often regret missing the opportunity to serve our nation. I suppose for selfish reasons. Perhaps that level of commitment was not in my DNA or I was just unwilling to go all in on something so much greater than myself. Maybe I was just lazy, lacked vision, courage, or discipline. These traits; commitment, courage, vision, selflessness, and discipline, which our midshipmen already embody, and are honing every day are the traits some adults, even the "best" among us, still struggle to master.

Our midshipmen sons and daughters, along with all the men and women who make up our U.S. military, are actively pursuing what so many of us want or need. The great news is it is within you; it is within all of us. We need to find the people, tools, and motivation to pull it out.

I believe our nation is suffering from a void of responsibility, accountability, and, collectively, is not the selfless America we once were. This life owes us nothing and there is no promise of tomorrow. Many in our country have become an entitled people and that has come to light in obscene ways. Peering through the veil of humanity, it seems as though our moral compasses are broken. There is a disconnect between right and wrong, an incongruence within our social structures, and no desire to live in truth.

Too many Americans do not understand the difference between rights and privileges. We are given the right to "pursue" happiness but never guaranteed it. Privileges can be taken away but never our rights as afforded under the Constitution.

Our military fights for these rights and our way of life every day and they understand the consequences. Like the T-shirt says, "Some people never meet their heroes. I raised mine." This is so true. As I know you are, I am so proud of what the Naval Academy stands for, the opportunity it is affording our children, and that I have a chance to watch how "pressure with a purpose" is molding our daughters.

I wonder, had I searched for the challenge so many years ago, would my life look different, for the good or worse for the wear? I will never know. However, I do know that we can all find that "warrior" mentality. We can look our enemy in the eye, whatever that might be for you, and kick tail like we care, not about ourselves, our feelings, or what others think of us, but for something greater than ourselves. Being willing to do so, no matter how hard it is, how much it hurts, or how uncomfortable it might be, is always the right thing to do.

# If the Game is Played, the Tailgate is On

Whether past, present, or future, there is a good chance anyone who proudly wears the fouled anchor on their cover has been blessed at the table of the New Jersey Parents Club tailgate which has faithfully served midshipmen meals at Navy Marine Corps Memorial Stadium since 1982. This is not a business; it is a ministry of sustenance to fill the hearts, minds, and stomachs of all those who don the uniform on game day. It has been coined "The Miracle on Asphalt," as no mid is left behind as each one seeking a meal leaves full and happy. My mother would be so proud.

What was started by Roy and Deb DeBore as a Navy tailgate with nothing more than an open car trunk which harbored enough food to only feed those mids who hailed from New Jersey is now an event even a food truck festival would envy. It is a colossal collection of approximately eighty volunteer parents who live the mantra "your mid is my mid" as well as anyone could. The New Jersey Parents Club dearly cares for and loves all those who toil on the Yard when Mom and Dad's reach is too short to be there. It is the gift that keeps on giving.

It is estimated approximately 1,000 mids are fed on game day, at no charge. Let that sink in for a moment. That is one big pantry. Tables and chairs sprawl out like large nets ready to capture the hunger of our superheroes. This NASCAR-like crew works with pit stop precision, the grill masters are organized like an Air Boss, and their hospitality committee greets each mid as if channeling the likes of Paula Deen. It is the only tailgate with its own Yelp site. It really is a spectacle to see!

This is not your grandmother's typical bridge club fare. The pleasing aromas that waft across the parking lot will bring the masses of those who wear summer whites and formal dress blues. The Naval Academy themed tents, banners, and spirit gear leave no doubt the passion our neighbors to the north have. They do what they do as well as anyone. Their menu reads like that of any fine diner and also includes international dishes which hail from Korea, Japan, and India, oh, my!

One of their delicacies and a crowd favorite is the Taylor ham, fried egg, and cheese sandwich, which I have had the distinct pleasure of tasting. Other menu items include, but are not limited to, pork roll sandwiches, steaks, hamburgers, chicken, Alabama chicken chili, pasta, desserts, and all the drinks one gullet can handle. I have been told they will even take requests on occasion. If they have the recipe, someone will endeavor to blend it, cook it, and serve it. It is a whole lotta luck in a pot and a grill full of love.

Being a southerner is no matter to this northern crew. They welcome all with open arms. I have seen it! There are too many loving souls to name who deserve praise for such culinary courage. Bill Asdal chairs the tailgate committee. His game day attendance is Navy strong at 110 (at time of printing) consecutive contests behind the scenes coordinating this historical event. He is faithful, like so many other parents are, to never let a kid go hungry or forgotten. He, like his cohorts, are true Navy angels.

These truly are remarkable people who deeply believe in their mission to serve our mids in a loving and thoughtful way. The photos on the website tell the story better than words can paint. Their labor goes unnoticed except by the hands and mouths of those who are the beneficiaries of their kindness each week when the boys in blue and gold suit up and take the field.

They do all this free of charge for our kids, but their costs are substantial (which are partly covered by other kind-hearted people who sacrificially give to ensure the tailgate will live on). I am just a North Carolina dad with two wonderful USNA daughters who has been bequeathed the joy this group brings to each game, and through that, my wife and I have been blessed.

To all the New Jersey mamas and the papas who have ever donned the apron of a sustenance warrior, "thank you" does not seem like enough. I am grateful for you, each of you. Though we may never meet, you are an example to so many. Even from afar, you have changed lives simply due to your giving hearts. Bless you all!

GO NAVY! BEAT ARMY!

# The Strength of the Anchor

My wife and I have seen sea deep truth in our two daughters' resolve, one newly commissioned and one a youngster. The Naval Academy is not for the faint of heart and it can be rough along the journey. However, the anchors they have found to steady their ship are their amazing midshipmen classmates and the USNA leadership. As I am shaking the ink in my quill today, hopefully you will find some truth in these words as well.

I believe each of us longs for a strong anchor to steady our ship whether in port or out at sea. But the tides, at times, can seem too high and the anchor chains too short to bed. Boxing the winds of change which can push us off course may follow with an order from a place not known within us to steer hard rudder right when we should have gone left. Often, when our keels are too short or the whitecaps too high, we know not which heading to bear. The horizon before us, which rises and falls, seems so vast and wide and lonely at times. As we feel the salty swill welling in our eyes, we hear the seaman say "Man overboard!" with each new tear that walks the plank.

Behold, a bright new day is dawning, leaving uncertainty and doubt behind. The moon bows down to the rising sun. The dark we fretted has sunk to the cavernous depths of the sea. Birds begin to lift to the air, tipping their wings to greet those sailors on early watch. Morning is here and the chill of night fades. The dolphins along the bow are nudging our ship to shore.

The crewmen manning the deck report the current is calm, no foe in sight. "Man the helm, steady the rudder!" says the captain. The compass is set, the heading is clear. But wait, what about our anchor? Is it still steady, is it still there? The wisdom of the COB speaks up. Our anchor is steady, it has remained faithful. We had but a weak link that struggled to serve. That link has now been forged by its brothers and sisters at arms. The team is tight, stronger than before. The sailor's heart, full of delight, cheers "Full steam ahead!" Our mission is complete.

Though the ocean journey was rough, and our anchor a bit unsure, we made it through the toils as good sailors should. Lengthen the chain and tether the ropes as the bulkhead bumps our long-trodden boat. We look left, and then right, and see our own anchors we love and left behind on the dock that dark night. But it is the anchors we sail with which will form a bond, a chain so tight, it will never break.

*Fair Winds and Following Seas*

# Chosen

This seemingly benign verb forever changed many young lives today. As if involved in tryouts for the varsity team, somewhere along Main Street USA, members of the Class of '22 were chosen to join a community they have worked towards for what seems like a thousand trips around the sun. Hearts are brimming, faces frozen with big toothy smiles, hugs seem warmer, and focus towards the future is becoming part of the new battle plan. However, I would be naïve to believe all the firsties who live in Bancroft are riding cloud nine tonight.

I only speak from my heart and draw on that which I have stuffed in my Mason jar of memories over our seven years as USNA parents. I have never served in uniform. I know not what it is like for my life to not be my own. My tenure as an American citizen, at least since high school, has been, in large part, sprinkled with delight in living life free of orders, commands, oaths, and, well, most anything dangerous. Only our finest one percent has raised their right hand to confirm they would put aside their lives to protect mine.

Tonight, there are approximately 1,000 young men and women who, after raising their courageous right hand on I-Day, are toeing the threshold of a Naval or Marine Corps career they thought may never come following the Plebe Summer shakedown. It has been a long journey across the seven seas, but they are almost ready to disembark the Naval Academy and enter new communities, which they have worked so hard for.

As USNA parents of capable and resilient children, I am often amazed, but never surprised, at the enormous gifts and talents they bring to the table of accomplishment. Their selfless hearts to serve the country represented by the stars and stripes patch they wear on their sleeves, our mids, though not exempt from disappointment, seem galvanized in their resolve to plant their feet where placed to fulfill their duty they so strongly believe in. Though a temporary punch in the gut may rise up following a second or third choice decision by those who sparkle with brass and silver, I believe those that stroll Stribling Walk each day will ready themselves to fight no matter the color of T-shirt they donned today.

Like you, I feel as though I need two hearts to hold the joy I feel for the class of '22. The opportunities that lie ahead will create the wake of their lives as they push the throttle down in pursuit of their dreams. May their keels remain plumb, their rudders straight, their subs run silent under the ocean blue, and their ground force be quick and true. I pray they will rise on lifted wings and win the battle in the valleys and celebrate victories from the mountaintop. Carry on, good and faithful sailor and Marine. HOOYAH! and OORAH! chants all around.

# Commissioning Week 2019 — Musings from the Bulkhead

During our daughter's commissioning week, I recall the ballast of my soul was heavy with blessings. Throughout the week, I often asked myself, "Why me, Lord? Why have You entrusted me to steward the things You have placed in my life? Things far greater than me." My basket was brimming with awe as I planted myself along the bulkhead and just watched our daughter's Naval Academy journey follow that long blue and gold line. I remember feeling honored God had invited me to the table of her life to observe His handiwork.

Driving home Saturday morning was bittersweet (mostly sweet with memories of the week we had left in our rearview mirror). So many of life's milestones had been trod upon, and accomplishments recognized, with congratulatory sentiments and lots of hugs. It was a time which will not soon be forgotten.

As my mind wandered down I-95, I realized I had just left a place so special, so sacred, that I wished all of our friends and family could have been there, right alongside, to experience the joy and delight of the moments embedded in one of the most glorious weeks of our and our daughter's lives. For those whose ticket was punched as they walked through the gates of

Navy-Marine Corps Memorial Stadium, and for the faithful who followed along virtually, I was thankful for all who sailed with us on that exciting three-hour tour which had a much happier outcome than that on television.

To the parents of future graduating classes, may you too find your own bulkhead to just sit and absorb this week. Amidst all the fanfare, celebration, pomp, and circumstance this week will offer, slow down, be still, and simply watch the majesty which will unfold before you. Your camera will capture your heart's love, but the harbor of your soul will overflow with your child's commitment to something greater than themselves.

# Pullin' Anchor

The Naval Academy is just hard. It is hard to get in and it is hard to get out. For some kids, it is a hard decision. The application process is hard. Induction Day is really hard. Plebe Summer is even harder. But midshipmen do hard things well. Many have never failed, at anything, ever. Their entire lives they have chosen not to approach life doing things the hard way, but instead, choosing to do the hard things in life, always with excellence. With that said, it leaves little wonder why our kids chose USNA.

Pullin' anchor is also hard. As parents, we have found solace within the USNA harbor along the Severn where our precocious lambs have diligently lived their mission statement to "develop midshipmen morally, mentally, and physically and to imbue them with the highest ideals of duty, honor, and loyalty." That is a high bar, but also a deeply embedded anchor of truth – an anchor which will be raised tomorrow, as each newly minted Navy Ensign and Marine Corps 2nd LT tosses their cover aloft led by three resounding "HIP, HIP, HOORAY!"

Their anchor will now have risen from the sand where it has dutifully laid since I-Day and we, their doting parents who raised these magnificent, though not perfect, young men and women, are now left standing on the dock as we wave bon voyage. Take heart, their compass is set, hull laid true, and the wake they leave will better those they lead.

Our 2019 LTJG is somewhere in the Pacific – we know not where. Mama prays every day for her baby who, not that long ago, wore smocked dresses and little Mary Janes. Ours has pulled her USNA anchor. She is now doing hard things in a hard world, but she chose the Navy, because like your midshipman, she has always chosen to do life this way.

# THE COVID CURSE

# Commissioning 2020 in 20/20

Our home's front door is a portal which has provided safe harbor for those who have entered through it for as long as our children can remember. One, a youngster, and the other, an ensign, have crossed this threshold many times, like passing through Narnia's wardrobe, to explore the wonders of what lies just beyond our front porch. It has been a passageway to climb new milestones, an opening for new beginnings, and a drop zone for loved ones and friends. Most days, it is like a liver as it humbly removes the impurities of our day. Our door has remained steadfast and true as it has protected those behind it and has been a thoroughfare of opportunity for any who sought it.

Commissioning Week for our '19 grad was akin to our front door. That week was like a portal for our mid as she moved from the relative safe harbor of the Naval Academy to the yet unknown currents of the fleet. As I watched each soon-to-be-commissioned officer walk proudly across the stage of great achievement, I could not help but see this moment as their wardrobe debut where, like Aslan, they were embarking on a mission to protect our great nation from the Wicked White Witch and those of her ilk that wish to do us harm.

As I read Superintendent Buck's COVID letter yesterday regarding commissioning week activities, my heart broke and my spirit wilted. One salty tear after another walked the plank of disappointment. How could this be? What was once the capstone of our daughter's USNA journey was now canceled for those who have followed? There will be no flyovers, cover toss, or first salutes. Our "Plebe No More" rendered her first to big sis. No pomp, circumstance, or parties to attend. Annapolis, typically brimming with military promise and proud families strolling the Yard, will be silent. The stadium, which has felt the triumph over its foes and endured the disappointment in its defeats, will not have felt such heartbreak as the loss associated with the absence of those who have worked so hard and long to relish in one last short walk.

Although the final door, which the class of 2020 will walk through, will look much different than their predecessors', the threshold over which they will step as they enter the field and fleet represents the same. The same door that slammed behind them on I-Day is now the door of new beginnings and great opportunity. The Naval Academy has done an honorable job of filtering the impurities out and refreshing our young leaders with courage, character, and a duty beyond self. Like our front door, on which hangs the anchor of strength, they will be steadfast and true to give safe harbor to those within and keep the wolf at bay. They will protect America's house.

Class of 2020, your mission is almost accomplished. Failure is not an option. As the battle space may change rapidly during your career, as it has now, your resiliency and adaptability in this time will be your hallmark while in uniform. Though COVID's backwash has drowned the hopes of commissioning week, my wish is our resolve will remain strong.

Parents ... you deserve CW. You are AMAZING! You have mixed all the special ingredients which have baked a pretty awesome cake. As my quill runs dry, please know my heart hurts for YOU. However, be encouraged. You have raised a hero who deserves a hero's send-off, ticker tape and all. Your mids will be okay. You, on the other hand, may need a bit more soothing. For me, CW was like watching my firstborn leave the comforts of my suburban grocery getter on the first day of kindergarten and then realizing I needed her more than she needed me.

# Not Just Another Drop in the COVID Bucket

Those of us who are of a certain age remember when life was not so automatic. Communication with friends and loved ones often meant dialing seven digits on a rotary phone, writing a letter with pen and paper, or using two tin cans tethered together was enough for my imagination. There were no smartphones, teleconferencing, social media, or Netflix to interrupt the solitude of life. Back then, we shook our pictures, recorded the Top Forty on cassette tapes, and sat on front porches to share the weekly gossip.

There was a time when our 2019 daughter and her betrothed fiancé, due to a newly COVID-induced restriction of movement, both soon to be submariners in Charleston's power school, learned their wedding plans had hit a bulkhead within a fortnight of their big day. Our daughter and her husband were married in Charleston, SC, not our hometown where a glorious fairytale wedding had been planned. As the coronavirus was beginning to dangle America from that famous cliffside tree in the movie "Cast Away," we created a new battle plan in an unfamiliar battle space. As any good field general would do, we rallied the troops and, with the swift surety of the wedding party, we planned a new, small wedding in seven days. It was a beautiful ceremony, in a beautiful setting, with beautiful people. As military life will prove itself to be challenging with regards to communication and time with our sailors and Marines, we have embraced our crash course in Zoom, Google Hangouts, and FaceTime. Thank heavens we had our youngster at home to help us navigate the tides of virtual relations.

In those times of social distancing, shelter in place orders, military travel bans, and mandatory whatchamacallits, I guess I am thankful for innovation. Although I still believe children should learn to write letters in cursive and make direct eye contact while speaking with others, I am learning to cherish the same technology which, in reality, has been causing some to social distance well before social distancing was considered cool. Without it, we might forget those faces only a mother could love.

Superintendent Buck's ROM letter, I am sure for most mid parents and loved ones looking forward to all USNA has to offer, including commissioning week, may have felt like a proverbial gut punch after already having both shins bruised. I am sure it broke Vice Admiral Buck's heart as well, as his mission to care for and protect the institution and all it stands for is an order which cannot be compromised. Hearts that had been pricked with disappointment are now open wounds of despair. The last thread of the unknown being held by the anchor of hope has been let loose. The ship seems to be sailing away and those who love their midshipman are left on the dock as they wave goodbye.

As much as our Navy family hurt for the class of 2020, as well as all midshipmen having to relinquish opportunities, in part, which defines the Naval Academy, as parents, we rejoice in our children's accomplishments. We applaud their accolades. We are grateful for their commitment. And we are in awe of their sacrifices. Peering through the fog of the bay as we navigate with only our compass in hand can be a bit unnerving. However, when the lighthouse of reassurance shines its beam upon our bow, my desire is we will find comfort in the guidance being given by our USNA leadership. Our soon-to-be-newly minted officers deserve the best as do you who are reading this now. It may be a virtual commissioning, but the feelings, emotions, and sense of accomplishment will be real. As the motto of the class of 2020 so cleverly coined, we all can cling to their words: "We will find a way or make one."

# The Thanksgiving COVID Consternation

Not since 2012, when Bill the mascot was goatnapped and tethered to a pole outside the Pentagon, have our beloved midshipmen, and us doting parents, had such a week of consternation.

Learning of the Thanksgiving liberty lockdown was like being served with withered stuffing, nestled on a bed of jelly-like canned cranberry sauce, and topped with congealed turkey gravy for the most anticipated dinner of the year. It was a sour forkful of reality to swallow, but should we drill down to our inner, deepest rational subconscious, even the most sentimental among us would confess all this COVID fussiness is for the greater good of the brigade. The USNA leadership is strong, capable, and they care deeply about our kids. Disagreement is allowed.

Plans have been altered, reservations canceled, and our collective souls have wilted like that of a poorly prepared green bean casserole. But we, as Academy tiger moms and helicopter dads, will surely rise up like the Pilgrims of old and embrace the suffering of separation, the despair of distance, and the loss of being with our loved ones on this uniquely American holiday.

I am sure those seasoned and salty Navy and Marine parents who have sailed these waters before us, although saddened by this unfortunate briefing of bad news, know the sea trials we are enduring will help prepare our hearts and minds for when our fledgling ensigns and second lieutenants ship out on long deployments. Holiday gatherings, birthday parties, and family vacations will no longer be guaranteed accessories that once adorned the lives of those who will soon serve.

Perhaps this holiday season of involuntary secession from our children will spin the first thread of placid fabric which will one day comfort our souls as we imagine which ocean, cloud, desert, or mountain range our sailors and Marines have touched that day. As parents, we signed the orders to pull anchor on I-Day as we watched, some with trepidation, our precocious offspring, clad in white from head to toe, march through those enormous bronze doors. It is times like these we must muster the courage to honor those orders.

Though big, long hugs are not on this year's Thanksgiving menu, nor the sweet dessert of a mama's love, I hope we can all find peace in knowing our mids have embarked on the right boat and their bow is pointed towards a bright future. Navigating heavy seas and taming turbulent currents is part of their journey. I believe it is part of ours as well. As John Paul Jones once proclaimed, "If fear is cultivated, it will become stronger. If faith is cultivated, it will achieve mastery."

Happy Thanksgiving to all and praying blessings on your mid this week. Your mid is my mid and we are all one big Navy loving family!

# Class of 2020 COVID Commissioning

Our rising 2nd Class mid recently quipped, "I-Day was the scariest day of my life." Her mother retorted, "Mine too!" My daughter and I snickered at her rapid fire response. My wife did not.

Reciting "I DO!" at the altar of holy matrimony shared by two betrothed souls is a commitment not to be entered into lightly. Much the same, a concert of newly minted plebes, right hands raised, as each one swears "I DO!" to uphold their oath of office, also understands this too is a commitment not to be entered into lightly.

"I" and "Do" are but two small words with a paltry three letters between them, yet when glued together, they represent the backbone of "thy word is truth," which galvanizes these dawning Navy and Marine Corps officers to harness the strength to carry the weight of our great nation on their collective backs. Their eager but anxious proclamation echoes around the hallowed granite and copper-laced walls of Bancroft Hall as Tecumseh watches over his court as if to say, "I got your six." It is at that precise moment the "I DOs" have it, and the U.S. Navy now has our children.

My advice, as a two-time I-Day veteran: Save yourself the embarrassment of becoming tear drunk until you are back within the safe confines of your vehicle, hopefully with dark tinted windows. Like a good margarita, be sure to mix in some joyful and sweet tears as those you are leaving behind are not only the best and brightest America has to offer, but you are also leaving them in the best and most capable hands the U.S. Naval Academy has to offer. Now would probably be a good time to go find that soothing margarita.

In spite of COVID, I have recently found great joy in celebrating with the commissioning class of 2020 via unexpected means, but given the circumstances, with a grateful heart. Like others of our ilk, I have embraced the idea of "ending it where it started." From white works on I-Day to formal whites on commissioning day, this is truly a "circle back" moment. As a good song can capture the essence of a place in time, the lyrics "ending it where it started," within the context of the class of 2020, would make for the richest ingredients to bake the most endearing love song ever written by anyone not named the Righteous Brothers.

To trod the same brick pavers, perch in the same white chairs, hoist the same right hand, catch the same reverberations of "I DO!" from the granite and copper-laced walls, and to know Tecumseh still has your six – what was once the scariest day of their lives – has become a day to celebrate a sense of accomplishment not known to anyone who has not, in unison, recited the full breakfast menu, including condiments, before the first rooster crowed. Their I-Day "I DOs" have become their commissioning day "I DIDs." It is a milestone day to cherish.

Congratulations, class of 2020! You deserve every single one tossed your way. Enjoy this time. You have earned it!

# 'Tis the Season

'Tis the season to rejoice in the small blessings we may not otherwise see amidst times of prosperity and plenty. This year has pressed upon us the wax seal of resolve when mercy seemed scarce. Though our shoulders have been burdened with the yoke of COVID misfortune, our galvanized hearts and determined souls have propped up our listing spirits.

As Naval Academy parents, I believe we have been fed but a small morsel of what life may look like as our fledging officers enter the fleet and field. Anchors will be pulled, ships will sail, and those charged with taking the fight to those who wish us ill will disappear into the deep, if only for a while. COVID has temporarily stripped us from the togetherness we so dearly covet, but the permanence of the love we have for our children and the pride which resides deep in our core will forever be the beacon which protects our ship from running aground in times of separation.

I pray each one of us will remember the small blessings thus far this year as we place upon the mantle of joy the moment our mid crosses the threshold into a home where the comfort it brings will be their sweetest blessing thus far, as well as it is ours.

Blessings to all, and to all, Fair Winds and Following Seas.

*ARMY-NAVY GAME*
*GO NAVY! BEAT ARMY!*

# A Game of Honor

⚓

"An adherence to what is right; high respect; great esteem" are but a few words my dictionary uses to describe "honor." The USNA mission, in part, reads, "to imbue them [midshipmen] with the highest ideals of duty, honor, and loyalty." Honor is not a word which should be taken lightly, but one reserved for those whose strength of character is wide enough to fill the battle uniform which hangs on the shoulders of our sons and daughters. Yes, indeed, being imbued with honor is no easy task, but one worth the early mornings, long days, and short nights frequently found on the Yard.

The word "honor" has also been set aside for the Army-Navy football game, an event unlike any other our nation has to offer. Its shoulders bear more weight than the Super Bowl and the feet upon which it stands have carried the ball of one of our best-loved traditions since 1890 – 121 times, thus far, someone has sung second.

The record between these two teams matters. The service academy who harbors the Commander-in-Chief's trophy matters. The men on the field who fight this contest between one another each year matters to so many. But what really matters is, though these two teams wear different jerseys, their uniforms don the same patch: our unfettered flag of freedom. Though their school colors are of a different hue, their purpose is of one mind. To "support and defend the constitution of the United States against all enemies, both foreign and domestic" is a truth which floats the moniker "A Game of Honor."

One sentence which, like a pillar of granite, upholds this pigskin classic that bears repeating every year, but never gets old, is "The Army-Navy Game is the only game where everyone playing is willing to die for everyone watching." I'd also like to add every cheerleader too! It is not a cliché, it's truth we, as parents, have embraced. It is the reality of those who are willing to lay down that which they cherish most, themselves. Saturday, December 11, is a big deal. Who sings second is a big deal. But those who proclaimed "I DO!" when many of us asked "Who will?" is an even bigger deal.

"May the best man win" is a polite show of sportsmanship, but in MetLife Stadium, all men between the white lines are winners simply because of who they were made to be.

GO NAVY! BEAT ARMY!

# America's Game

The time to target is near. Our battle groups are poised to sail the Hudson. The Navy Jack and the Gadsden flag ("Don't Tread on Me") fly high upon the jackstaff. Saturday is the day two formidable foes will battle, as if John Paul Jones and George S. Patton were standing toe-to-toe with pride for country on one shoulder and a duty to defeat their enemy on the other. Like Navy SEALs, who come shrouded by night, so too will Coach Niumatalolo and his mighty band of brothers be mission focused, hardened by their will to win.

History has testified that a fissure runs deep through the collective blood of these two institutions and those who align their allegiance with others of their ilk. But cadets and midshipmen, soldiers, sailors, Marines, parents, in-laws, outlaws, loved ones, and all Americans alike, from the highest mountain peaks to the lowest coastal plains, have a sense, as if it has been sewn into our DNA, that this is a special day. A day where those sworn to fight as one will fight one another for the privilege to sing second.

The memes have made us grin, the spirit spots tickled our senses, and we have sobbed while watching reruns of CBS teaser films. And yes, it does "take a different kind of kid" – a kid with a heart to serve, an intellect to lead, and a will to protect against those who wish us harm. The truth still remains, every player between the lines is willing to die for every soul standing outside the lines.

Amidst the pomp and circumstance, majestic march-on, chilling flyover, and historic coin toss, nothing will compel my heart on game day more than the angelic Army-Navy glee club's rendition of our national anthem, a sound of freedom no foe can put asunder. Our patriotic spirits will stand at attention, hands hovering over our hearts, some at full salute, with our resolve glued together as one nation, under God, indivisible against our enemies, both foreign and domestic, and in pursuit of justice for all. HOOYAH! and OORAH!

We can throw the win-loss record out with yesterday's boxed lunch. Though the boys in blue and gold are 16-5 since the turn of the century, the only numbers that will matter Saturday are those on the scoreboard. As the sun sets and renders its salute to the rising moon, a victor will emerge. The battle for bragging rights will have ended. But this battle is like none other afield. The only casualties on the gridiron will be bloodied elbows, bruised muscles, and, for one team, a concussion of egos.

Who will sing second? That's the mission. The orders have been given to defeat their foe. One team will emerge the victor and embrace the spoils of their impending football war. The fierce fight will soon end, and like brothers in arms, these young men, and women too, will rally once again, as one unit for global good. Our pride will swell and our deep admiration for our nation's officers in training will grow. Win or lose, the lessons learned on the field will churn in the souls of these young men forever. For me, a truer statement could not be made about this monumental contest. It is indeed "America's Game."

GO NAVY! BEAT ARMY!

# "I Have Not Yet Begun to Fight"
# Captain John Paul Jones

If I were an American foe, I would beg not to fall beneath the cannons of such a battle cry. Those early warriors of land and sea, who served under the growing shadow of our unfettered fabric of freedom, have carved a path across the annals of military heroism for each of us to remember.

Tomorrow, our blue and gold heroes, some who we raised inch by inch, will engage in a battle of bragging rights, both from the field and standing side-by-side, seat-by-seat.

The march-on will be a promenade of force. The mid-field meeting is a promise of fair play, but Navy's shot across the bow will be felt, like thunder, deep in the bowels of all those who witness the Blue Angels make their presence known when they "buzz the tower" of MetLife Stadium.

The sound of freedom will pass above powered by a love of country and a dedication to protect her against all enemies, both foreign and domestic. It is then our hearts will rise with reverence to the pigskin combat before us. Our mission is clear, resolve unwavering, and a will to win will well up in us to proclaim from the ship's bridge the battle cry our formidable Navy hero once retorted amidst cannon fire and chaos. For this day, we will twist Captain John Paul Jones's retort just a bit to fit the circumstance.

We are now ready to fight!

GO NAVY! BEAT ARMY!

# A SERVICE SALUTE

# A Salute to Our Midshipmen

Each time I stumble upon a photo of our mids while scrolling through my camera roll, the reminiscent puppeteer, who resides somewhere deep in my memory tank, gently pulls on my heart strings as if to nudge my thoughts backwards to a time when something uniquely special had happened. A photo I recently crossed of twin girls, approximately eight years old, wearing Navy swag, offering a complimentary salute to our then youngster, was such a time.

I cannot recall who rendered the first salute, but I will not soon forget the significance of this moment. Perhaps my daughter knew, as a young lady in uniform, this simple gesture of respect donated to those of her kind, although some may consider it child's play, meant something greater to these precocious twin kiddos.

As Naval Academy parents, some of us can pinpoint the day our eager offspring declared their intent of becoming a midshipman. While that declaration is a bit fuzzy for others, we all knew that once the sun rose over Alumni Hall on I-Day, they were in the right place and were ready to accept the challenge of Plebe Summer, though some of our little lambs, with a bit less hair, may have felt differently by sunset.

I often wonder from where the inspiration flows that infuses our children with the heart of selfless service, a sacrificial soul, and with great courage, long to lend solace in times of immense stress. I have a hunch it is their life's heroes who have spun the thread our aspiring Navy and Marine Corps officers have used to knit together one unfettered piece of blue and gold fabric they proudly fly as they drive into Annapolis on their big day. Lessons they have learned along the way, even those born from mischief which may remain in their secret vault, at least until the statute of limitations has expired, once sewn together, have created a beautiful tapestry that represents a life well lived and a well-honed body, mind, and spirit.

Parents, you too have helped to weave your own beautiful tapestry using the yarn of love, sacrifice, dedication, and a never give up attitude your kids desperately needed. Those carpools, plays, band competitions, recitals, athletic events, church camps, the volunteer hours you logged, and all the times you broke bread together around the kitchen table all mattered. Although they may not say it, you are most likely your mid's most important life's hero. It is the yarn of the everyday, seemingly mundane moments of life you have used to weave your own tapestry, except this one may never be seen as it will wrap the hearts and souls of your mid for their four years on the Yard and into the fleet.

A proverbial salute from those we admire, in any form, can be the spark needed to set our compass on a course to greatness. One good seed can bear great fruit. My hope is this one small gesture of kindness, a simple salute and smile, will be a seed of many sown along the row by those who care for these two little ones. Whether their dreams are to attend the Naval Academy or explore another worthy path, like our kids, their parents will be their number one hero just like our mids have become ours.

# The National Museum of the Marine Corps

Captain C.W. Morgan, U.S. Navy, once said, "The Marines will never disappoint the expectations of their country – NEVER!"

Wow! That's a whole peck of comfort and pride baked into this pronouncement of courage and commitment. Capt. Morgan spoke truth when he quipped these words almost 160 years ago and they still bear truth today.

Not being a U.S. Marine, but a friend of a few and the dad of two USNA daughters, this thread of military fortitude sews together my heart with those who have fought and died on my behalf and on that of this great country we call home. They expect little from us, their compatriots, but our expectations of them drives their instinct to protect and serve.

There are only two people who are willing to sacrifice their own lives for the betterment of others. One was Jesus Christ, and the other? Those who don the uniform of honor pasted with patches of their units, squadrons, medals of wars fought, accolades of well-earned exploits, and the unfettered flag of freedom.

I am not the one for whom these words were chiseled in stone, but instead they are on display to coincide with the permanence of the memory of those this museum was created to remember.

In an effort to drop wisdom, such as this, in the blender of truth, hoping to spin Captain Morgan's words to find application for my own life, someone who has never felt the pain of war or the loss of souls on the battlefield, I set aside a few moments to ponder on that which spilled from the pitcher into my cup of courage. Here is what I was able to string together...

"I may disappoint the expectations of those who have sacrificially poured themselves into my life, but I will never cease being grateful to them for creating in me a pitcher of desire to pour into others – NEVER!"

We will NEVER forget those who perish at the hands of senseless evil, nor will the hundreds of thousands of Americans for which museums such as these were erected. May we pour ourselves into the lives of our military and into the lives of their families who may be left behind.

# Veterans Day and Those Yet to Come

As Naval Academy parents, the ballast of pride we harbor in our hearts is often more than we can carry. We feel compelled to tell the story of the offer of appointment to our friends and family, what it means and how, upon receipt, it forever changed the lives of those their mothers gave birth to. But if you are like most of us, this magical story can be told but not fully understood by those who have not untied their own bowline and pushed back the boat of separation. We watch our young people proclaim "I DO!" then march, about face, through huge bronze doors which seem two stories tall only to be slammed in our faces. Once the eyes glaze over of the person's ear I am bending, it is time to stop talking as we have just spun the Wheel of Fortune. My polite listener can no longer solve the puzzle which reads "YOU GOTTA SEE IT TO BELIEVE IT."

Brevity is not a gift I possess, but I will press on to my point. Though our current USNA kids have yet to be christened to sail into the fleet or endured TBS as they become galvanized Marines, they will one day receive the honor due to our service veterans. Whether they serve their five or push forward to twenty-five, our gratitude should be palpable.

"I do solemnly swear that I will support and defend the Constitution of the United States against all enemies, foreign and domestic" is a ruck sack full of promise my back has never had to carry, but I am forever indebted to those who have. I cannot understand, empathize, or relate to those who have served. To do so would betray my character. To hold up our service members and veterans in high regard, with a thankful heart and celebratory mind, is my best gift to those who don the uniform of the day.

My hope is that same ballast of pride which I harbor in my heart for our squared away midshipmen will be poured out for those who return home, most less whole than when they deployed. Many veterans want to tell their stories while others cannot seem to find the words. Sadly, our heroes marked by marble stones have been forever silenced, but not forgotten, and will always be cherished.

For those who have stood at the door and kept the wolf at bay to protect those who cannot protect themselves, thank you! You are an American treasure. The sword you carry, whether into battle or behind a shore duty desk, matters. Our great country is indebted to your sacrifice. The question you once asked with great valor – "If not me, then who?" – is one most of us would never dare trod upon.

Our military is the best friend any nation could have but is also its worst enemy. Those that came before us knew what that meant. Our veterans took their "obligation freely, without any mental reservation or purpose of evasion." They trained for it and executed their mission to the best of their abilities on behalf of you and me.

So, USNA parents, though our Navy theater programs are firmly in hand, tomorrow's page is void of the next act. We only see today's scene in play. The ship is sailing, but we know not where. The sails have been hoisted, but we cannot see. The command has been shouted from the bridge but we cannot hear. The heroes we raised now saunter down Stribling Walk as they begin to parlay their future as Navy and Marine Corps officers.

While I am becoming a really good cheerleader from the bulkhead of Navy life, I am also practicing not only how to be a good storyteller but also an intent listener. When a veteran needs an ear to bend someday, though I may not solve their puzzle, I pray the ballast of pride which finds safe harbor in my heart will be poured out, freely, as if to say, "I am proud of you. Well done, good and faithful servant."

# Living in the Wake of the Evacuation of Afghanistan

Our family's home is nestled in a place where violence is scant and peace overflows from our cups of milk and honey. Apple pie courses through our veins and pride for our great nation hangs from our front porch. We believe our flag is unfettered and represents freedom which has been secured by our brave men and women who have fought for it, even died for it, but for little acknowledgement in return.

As I retired to my study last evening, I wept as the burden of the hamster wheel of the day's military news lay heavy on my shoulders. I wept for the guilt I felt for the comfort that surrounded me. My fridge and pantry are full, my home is air conditioned, my couch is comfortable, and the four walls of our home would not be breached by those wishing us harm simply because of our gender, faith, or politics. We are blessed beyond measure. And then, an imaginary mortar penetrated my spirit. I looked up and saw framed photos of our two daughters, one a firstie and the other a sub officer. I wept again, and I prayed. "God, may your hand of protection and mercy be upon them, their classmates, and all those who fight to stare down Satan's work in this world. I lift up our Afghan brothers and sisters and all those who are crying for a savior tonight. Amen."

Our eleven Marines, one Army soldier, and one Navy corpsman who perished at the hands of evil yesterday at Kabul Airport were sacrificial spools who have given their patriotic thread, now stitched into the bright stars and red and white fabric which now represent the thirteen stripes of our grand and glorious American banner. Their families will be given a gold star, a star they never wished for. A vacant seat, a muted voice, and one less birthday to celebrate together. It's a reality we as military parents live with, but try to ignore. The thirteen sets of parents who will receive folded flags to honor the passing of their mighty warriors will forever grieve their loss and wish for their return. I do not believe God intended that we outlive our children.

Afghan children seem to delight in our soldiers – those who come, as if angels in battle dress uniforms, to protect and shelter them from the worst of what our world has to offer. Unconditional love and service beyond self is an idea unrivaled and not seen by many Afghan people. The people smile when life offers them little to smile about. Their children exude joy in an era when the world seems joyless. And parents have hope for future generations when hope seems scarce. I pray for their souls as their future now seems bleak. I pray that God will reach down and calm their fear and deliver them from evil. I pray my heart will be softened if I complain when the drive-thru line is too long. Amen.

Though our flag is unfettered, today it feels a bit tattered. Though our resolve is strong, our spirit has been a bit weakened. Though our military is like a legion of Spartans, we feel the loss of thirteen as strongly as if they were our last. I am not confident we know how this ends, but God does. However, I do know your kids, my kids, and every soul who said "I will support and defend the Constitution of the United

States against all enemies, foreign and domestic" are ready to determine its outcome. We must remain strong to fight, diligent to protect, and mad as hell to deliver justice to those who hurt us.

# A Tale of Fireworks and the Humorous Side of American Freedom

Celebrating the fourth day of July or, for the history buffs amongst us, Independence Day, is not so much about the calendar day upon which this holiday falls, but rather what it represents.

I am not a huge fireworks lover. I know this may be considered un-American by some. However, I do love barbecue, hotdogs, casseroles, miniature Stars and Stripes flags, and those little patriotic sugar cookies with red, white, and blue sprinkles that accompany this fine holiday.

However, did you know our beloved mid-summer extravaganza is fraught with unintended consequences? For instance, sparklers, often introduced to our children at an impressionable age, are considered within the Pyrotechnics Council of America as a gateway pyrotechnic, much like marijuana is a gateway drug, that can lead to more dangerous incendiary devices. These include, but are not limited to, bottle rockets, lady fingers, M-80s, and heaven forbid your little sweetheart grab a hold of a Roman candle. Though they do make for fun battle gear. There is nothing more senseless than losing a finger due to the improper use of good black powder and kerosene.

Instagram posters unite! Tonight will be your crowning moment to snap those rockets red glaring and bombs bursting. Capturing those brilliant hues of red, orange, blue, and green is not for the novice iPhone photographer. I am sure, by the dawn's early light, our timelines will be dripping with out-of-focus shots of skyward explosions rivaled only by the picture quality of your parents' Polaroid camera.

Parties everywhere! I have always admired our country's patriotism through the conduit of peaceful displays of camaraderie for a common cause. Heck, if there is a soirée to be had, Americans will celebrate anything, even the monumental events of foreign lands such as Cinco de Mayo. July Fourth, for some of our more ambitious citizens, is a time of year for simply another excuse to gather around the smoker's pit of life, hoot, holla, drink beer, and drink more beer. (Coolers allowed but no glass bottles, please.) And remember, good decision making begins at the brew thru when you opt for the twelve pack, not the twenty-four.

And, who could forget the Godfather of American anthems on this day of patriotic celebration? I am a lover, not a fighter. I have been known to let slip a tear or two while under the spell of sweet clover honey and Granny's apple pie. Had Lee Greenwood been walking upright in 1776, I feel certain he would have signed the Declaration of Independence right along with our other founding fathers. I just cannot help myself, "God Bless the USA" makes me cry drunk every time. Somehow, I find embarrassing myself in front of total strangers for the love of country is okay.

Y'all hooligans down the street with the firework multi-pack you bought at Wal-Mart, just stop it. Even with her thunder shirt on, my dog is over here having a conniption.

But really, let us all remember why we celebrate Independence Day. It was not just a day, it was a movement. We owe our freedom to so many great Americans, starting with the colonists who dreamed of a better life when they fled the oppressive monarchy and achieved it at great risk to themselves and their families. The British royalty was no match for Paul Revere and his mighty steed. The Redcoats tried to take our guns, so we shot them. The Declaration of Independence was the most epic "Dear John" letter ever written.

Francis Scott Key penned it best after witnessing the British bombardment of Fort McHenry. Key was inspired by one lone U.S. flag still flying over the fort at daybreak. He surmised our resolve cannot be broken, and our fabric of freedom cannot be unwoven. This poem, in part, put to music, describes the genesis of our American spirit and why we look upon in such awe each July Fourth at our local firework show.

*And the rockets' red glare, the bombs bursting in air,*
*Gave proof through the night that our flag was still there.*
*Oh, say does that star-spangled banner yet wave*
*O'er the land of the free and the home of the brave.*

I give thanks for our USNA kids who are preparing themselves to fight for the very same freedom our fledgling country did all those centuries ago. They truly are becoming the American heroes we raised them to be.

# ABOUT THE AUTHOR

Steve Wade and his wife Mary Jane spent many days perched on the bulkhead along the Severn as they watched both their daughters ('19 and '22) navigate life as U.S. Naval Academy midshipmen. Steve has journaled his observations throughout his seven years visiting the Yard.

This book is an insightful compilation of his humorous ponderings and heart piercing stories told from a parent's perspective. You will find inner truth in Steve's writing which will bring water balloon tears of hope and joy as you reflect on your own future Navy or Marine Corps officer. If you have worn white works, service dress blues on parade or walked along Stribling in summer whites, may these writings bring good memories and bear truth as you look back on your time as a midshipman. There is a good chance you will also find a whole barrel of pride in who your children are becoming and the years of hard work and prayer which helped set them on their course.

## Review Requested:

We'd like to know if you enjoyed the book.
Please consider leaving a review on the platform
from which you purchased the book.

CPSIA information can be obtained
at www.ICGtesting.com
Printed in the USA
BVHW041420160423
662363BV00007B/550

9 781682 356203